TO THE OTHER SHORE

TO THE OTHER SHORE

Lalla's Life and Poetry

Vitastā
New Delhi

First published in India by Vitasta, New Delhi

ISBN: 81-86588-06-X

Produced by Tulika Print Communication Services
35A/1, Third Floor, Shahpur Jat, New Delhi - 110 049

Printed at Pauls Press
E 44/11 Okhla Phase II, New Delhi - 110 020

For
my mother and late father

Contents

Preface

LALLA has inspired Kashmiris of all religions through the beauty and wisdom of her poetry which was orally transmitted for centuries. Her verses are aphoristic in nature but with a musicality which is hard to capture in translation. Lalla left such a permanent mark on Kashmiri language and culture, that her legacy has survived innumerable political upheavals and religious conflicts.

Lalleshwari, to use Lalla's formal name, was born in a brahmin family, but her verses have been treasured by Kashmiris of all faiths. She especially captured the folk imagination of generations of women. My old aunts who grew up in Kashmir have memories of women reciting Lalla's verses in melodious voices while they worked at the spinning wheel. Later day women mystics, too, talked of Lalla and her verses to their mixed male and female audience. Women, especially those who faced oppressive domestic situations, often discovered their own inner strength through her words. Lalla's words were daily used to corroborate a point or to say what the speaker was unable to express in her own words.

Lalla in time became the wise old woman of Kashmiri culture and was invoked not only at moments of personal dilemma but also to celebrate moments of social togetherness. I myself remember my mother singing Lalla's verses and quoting them in her conversations. Women poets who followed Lalla drew their inspiration from her. For example, Rupa

Bhavani (1625–1721), another famous Kashmiri poet/mystic, calls Lalleshwari as the teacher who embodied knowledge and whose very essence was purity and tranquillity (Dhar 30). Ninety six verses composed by Rupa in mixed Kashmiri and Sanskrit are as similar to Lalla's in their content as Rupa's life was to Lalla's in her asceticism. Rupa was also regarded as a social reformer who worked hard to stop polygamy amongst the Kashmiri brahmin community because she felt it was unjust to women.

No recent critical work is available on Lalleshwari, except a study done by Jayalal Kaul which clarifies some of the misconceptions, especially with respect to the Kashmiri Shaiva basis of her thinking. New insights can be gathered from Lalla's life and work by applying recent feminist scholarship from India and the West to better understand her as a historical figure with significance for contemporary women.

The purpose of the current study is twofold—first to locate Lalla, the historical person, in medieval Kashmir. This requires a brief discussion of the socio-political conditions of the fourteenth century Kashmir. Exploring the familial and institutional structures of that period indicates that it must have been very hard for a woman interested in exploring metaphysical questions to operate from within the patriarchal social formations. The sociological inquiry into medieval Kashmir thus reveals the nature of Lalla's relationship to her family and community and provides an insight into the constraints that shaped her material existence. Lalla lived during a time of great political changes. The rulership of Kashmir which was in the hands of Hindu kings for centuries finally passed on to Muslim Sultans. The change in rulership created fundamental transformation in social equations. This was also the time when Sufism began to make inroads into the social imagination. It is beyond the scope of the present study to explore the relationship of Lalla's thought to Sufism. My inquiry is limited to the role

Kashmir Shaivism played in shaping her attitudes and beliefs which helped her transcend standard religious categories and socially defined gender roles.

In so far as Indian metaphysical theories come with sets of practices, Kashmir Shaivism too has a set of practices which, according to tradition, lead to the experience of the reality about which it theorizes. My exploration here into Kashmiri Shaivism in general, and Lalla's verses in particular, does not aim to negate the immediate ontological experience which Shaiva metaphysics propounds. It rather attempts to show that the nature of this experience is strongly determined, in its first stages, by the specificity of gender and class. I also critique the descriptions of this reality which are pervasively male-centered. I argue that Lalla's interest in the Kashmir Shaiva tradition which she practiced very seriously was deepened due to her disenchantment with the conditions of her material existence. As a woman, she probably did not have access to the written tradition of the Shaiva philosophy. The male members of her social class had access to these texts by means of which they sought to ensure the continuity of their thinking and lives. Lalla, on the other hand, could find no such continuity in the male tradition of Kashmir Shaivism and had to establish her own inner connection with the truths to be found there. Her involvement in the tradition was based on her personal experience rather than any elaborate study of texts. She transmitted Shaiva teachings to the common people in vernacular Kashmiri language, so that they were accessible not only to the male and female members of her own community, but also to the outsiders. My analysis finally reveals that Lalla's asceticism was due to her location as a woman practitioner within the Kashmiri Shaiva tradition. This location placed her spiritual attainment in a contradictory position to the traditional role of a woman and a wife in which self-effacement and subservience rather than self-mastery were promoted. Lalla's verses, then, represent the female voice that re-presents and finally transforms a male-centered model of reality. Her verses metaphorically express the experiences of a journeying self on its way to increasing awareness.

My work on Lalla's verses has been a great source of joy and personal fulfillment for me as it has allowed me to pursue my deep interest in Kashmiri Shaiva thought from a woman's perspective. I thank the University of Hawaii's Research Relations Office that provided me a grant to travel to India to do research on Lalla in the Summer of 1992. My special thanks to Peter Manicas, Director of the Liberal Studies Program at the University of Hawaii, who allowed me to take time off to travel to India. He has been a special colleague and a mentor throughout the time when I was working on this manuscript. My heartfelt gratitude goes to my late father, Ram Nath Kak, a Kashmiri scholar, who went over my translation of the verses and shared with me his unique knowledge of the Shaiva tradition. This project would have been inconceivable without my mother Sarojini Kak whose stories brought Lalla alive to me. Finally, the foundation for this work was laid by the late Kashmiri Shaiva scholar and teacher Swami Lakshman Jee who ignited the spark to pursue my interest in Kashmiri Shaivism and has been a source of inspiration for me for many years. My sister and brothers—Shakti, Avinash, Subhash, and Neeraj—are all indelibly stamped on the pages of this book. Both Shakti and Subhash commented on various drafts of the manuscript which helped bring it to its final form. My son Vajra contributed to the work in his own way as he patiently accustomed himself to hot Indian summers and long conversations on Lalla in Kashmiri many years in a row. Lalla became the enigmatic figure of his childhood imagination. I am grateful to Joseph Singer for numerous enlightening discussions on literature and art over the years and for his many helpful comments as he carefully read the manuscript. The manuscript benefited greatly from Alex Kiriako's invaluable editorial suggestions and I thank him for that. Finally, I feel deep gratitude for Kumkum Sangari for asking important questions and giving useful suggestions as she carefully read the final draft of the manuscript.

Hawaii JAISHREE KAK ODIN

Abbreviations

SS *Aphorisms of Shiva: The Siva Sutra with Bhaskara's Commentary, the Varttika*. Trans. Mark S.G. Dyczkowski.

AB Masson, J.L. and M.V. Patwardhan. *Santarasa and Abhinavagupta's Philosophy of Aesthetics.*

DL *The Dhvanyaloka of Anandavardhana.* With the *Locana* of Abhinavagupta. Trans. Daniel H. H. Ingalls, Jeffrey M. Masson and M.V. Patwardhan.

JRT Jonaraja. *Rajatarangini of Jonaraja.* Trans. Jogesh Chunder Dutt.

KRT Kalahana. *Rajatarangini.* Trans. R.S. Pandit.

KS *Koshur Samachar. Lal Ded Number.*

LV Sir George Grierson and Lionell D. Barnett. *Lalla Vakyani.*

SP *The Siva Purana.* Vols. 1–4. Ed. J. L. Shastri.

SV *The Stanzas on Vibration.* Translation of *Spandakarikas* and various commentaries by Mark S. G. Dyczkowski.

VB *Vijnanabhairava or Divine Consciousness.* Trans. Jaideva Singh.

CHAPTER ONE

Introduction

LALLA'S aphoristic verses have been an integral part of Kashmiri culture for over six centuries. The oral transmission of her compositions over a prolonged period of time illustrates the extent to which she has been a part of the folk memory. Her verses, originally uttered in old Kashmiri, are filled with vivid images that capture thoughts and experiences of her life. She employs the imagery and metaphors of daily life to convey to common people her vision of reality, in order to provoke them to look beyond the veil of inhibitions and constraints imposed by societal institutions. In the feudal society of her time when the majority of people were preoccupied with the simple act of survival, her verses challenged them to experience the source of empowerment from within based on spirituality rather than religious dogmatism.

As is common with any oral tradition, it is hard to imagine that her verses come to us without any change. Not only were they subject to changes in the language itself, but also to reinscription as the society changed. The additions, deletions, and reinscriptions were probably minimal because of a very strong oral tradition in medieval Kashmir where some brahmin families specialized in the rote memorization of oral or written texts which were passed on from the teacher to disciples, or within the family from one generation to another.

Collections of Lalla's verses have been compiled from time to time by various individuals. The first scholarly collection of Lalla's verses in the West was put together by Sir George Grierson and Lionell D. Barnett in 1920. They wrote about their inability to get an authentic manuscript of her verses. The manuscripts that they found were either incomplete or no two matched in content or text. However, they do point out that even in the absence of authentic manuscripts, it was possible for them to compile a fairly accurate text of Lalla's verses based on various sources which included meticulous records of oral tradition. Grierson and Barnett discovered that "the ancient Indian system by which literature [was] recorded not on paper but on the memory, and carried down from generation to generation of teachers and pupils, [was] still in complete survival in Kashmir" (LV 3). Commenting further on the tradition of oral transmission in Kashmir, they relate Aurel Stein's experience in collecting Kashmiri folk tales from a professional storyteller in the summer of 1896. Stein wrote down the folk tales as told by the storyteller word for word. He soon found out that there were a number of words in the tales that the narrator did not understand. When pressed to explain the meaning of the words, the narrator insisted that this is how he had received the tales and he did not know their meaning. These tales were simultaneously recorded by a learned Pandit who also did not understand the meaning of some of the words, but nonetheless accepted them unquestioningly on the authority of the narrator. Fifteen years later, at Grierson's request Stein asked the reciter to repeat the passages with these words: the retelling was "*verbatim, literatim, et punctatim*," as it was recited to him years ago. This incident, Grierson and Barnett point out, shows beyond doubt that a well-developed system of oral transmission existed in Kashmir where some families for religious or other reasons saw it as their duty to pass on meaningful texts to the next generations. Thus, the "reciters, even when learned Pandits, [took] every care to deliver the messages word for word as they [had] received them, whether they under[stood] them or not. In such cases we not infrequently come across words of which the meaning given is purely traditional or is even lost" (LV 3).

According to Grierson and Barnett, their collection of Lalla's verses was acquired under similar conditions. In 1914, Pandit Mukunda Rama Shastri recorded for Grierson an authentic collection of Lalla's verses from an old brahmin named Dharma-dasa Darwesh in the village of Gush who recited these verses to community members as part of his family tradition. In this recension, too, there were words and expressions that the reciter did not understand. The reciter could have easily changed the unintelligible words but did not do so because this is how he had received them.

In addition to this collection, Grierson and Barnett also consulted two other manuscripts of the Stein collection at the Oxford Indian Institute, Stein A and Stein B, both written in the Sharada alphabet of Kashmir. The first manuscript, Stein A, is a fragment, the first two leaves and all those following the seventeenth are missing. The verses in this fragment include the original text of forty one verses along with their Sanskrit translation by a Kashmiri Pandit called Rajanaka Bhaskara. A complete edition of Rajanaka Bhaskara's translation of sixty verses in Sanskrit was printed in Kashmir when Grierson and Barnett were compiling their collection. This edition was used by them to supply the missing verses of the Stein A collection. The second manuscript, Stein B, includes the Kashmiri text of forty nine of the verses included in the Grierson collection. However, it has yet to be established how old these manuscripts are or whether they are copies of original manuscripts that were written earlier. Rajanaka Bhaskara's translation has been dated to be around two hundred years old when it was reprinted in Kashmir. Aside from Grierson and Barnett's 109 verse collection in *Lalla Vakyani*, Pandit Anand Koul collected a number of verses, out of which he considered seventy five to be authentic and these were published in the *Indian Antiquary* in the 1930s.

Over the decades, the scholars of Lalla's work have regarded Grierson collection of 109 verses as the most authentic available collection. In a recent critical study *Lal Ded*, Jayalal Kaul too admits that except for a few verses, "on the whole, ...(the Grierson collection has) succeeded in giving us an authentic text" of Lalla's verses (30–31). Kaul's study of Persian sources sheds further light on the confusion related to some of Lalla's verses. The Persian sources are important since some of Lalla's verses seem to have been mixed up with those of the Sufi mystic Sheikh Nur-ud-din who lived during Lalla's time and greatly revered her. Kaul notes thirty five verses in various Lalla collections are also part of *Nurnama-s* and *Rishinama-s*, the biographies of Sheikh Nur-ud-din. Many of these in later copies of the *Rishinama-s* have been wrongly attributed to Nur-ud-din, even though this mixing-up of verses is not present in the earlier copies (Kaul 40). Since we have no concrete evidence to show whether the Lalla manuscripts or copies of manuscripts, the basis of Grierson collection, were written before or after the earliest *Nur-nama* recorded two hundred years after Sheikh Nur-ud-din's death, one cannot ascertain the true originator of the handful of verses that have been attributed both to Nur-ud-din and Lalla. Ultimately, it is the style of the verses that determines their validity.

Rahman Rahi notes that even though verses by the two resemble each other superficially, they are vastly different in their style. He describes Lalla'a verses as "live embers, while the Sheikh's *shrukh* are like sparks in dying ashes. The background may almost be the same, but in the process of poetic creation, something has intervened which accounts for the wide difference between the poetry of the mystic poets." Rahi adds further that Nur-ud-din's verses are more in the form of moral lesson rather than depiction of a deep experience, with the result they "do not penetrate and stir the heart. The similes and metaphors he employs are illustrative and explanatory, they do not become live symbols for a deeply felt experience."[1]

The same criteria can in fact be used to distinguish Lalla's verses from those that are spurious additions or variations—quite a number of which are present in Anand Koul's collection. The collection of 148 verses presented here, is based on Grierson and Barnett's *Lalla Vakyani*, Anand Koul's 75 verse collection published in the *Indian Antiquary*, and *The Wise Sayings of Laleshwari* by S. N. Charagi. In addition, I have also consulted the collection of verses in Jayalal Kaul's *Lal Ded* as well as in *Koshur Samachar* (1971). I reject verses numbered 89, 90, 91, 92, 99 and 100[2] in Grierson collection because these do not conform to Lalla's style. I also did not consider several verses from other collections which did not depict Lalla'a mastery of metaphoric expression. Several verses in Anand Koul's collection appear to be either variants or later additions. The collection of verses in *Koshur Samachar* is a compilation from several different sources, but here, too, a great number can easily be rejected since they do not conform to the style or thought content that we have come to associate with Lalla. The concordance at the end of my collection is based on Grierson and Barnett's *Lalla Vakyani*, Anand Koul's collection of 75 additional verses that were published in the *Indian Antiquary* (Vols L, LIX, LX, LXI, LXII), Jayalal Kaul's *Lal Ded* collection, and my own Lalla collection of 148 verses. Even though Jayalal Kaul's collection only gives the first line of each verse in Kashmiri, I have included it in the concordance because of the depth and rigor of the scholarship that he exhibits in his *Lal Ded*, especially with respect to the Persian sources.

[1] Rahman Rahi, *Koshur Shiraza*. Quoted in Kaul 39–40.

[2] According to Jayalal Kaul, verse 99 and 100 of the Grierson collection are from an early nineteenth century Kashmiri gazal by Aziz Khan.

Lalla's compositions, originally narrated in old Kashmiri, come to us in a form that is fairly modern, except for occasional archaic expressions with obscure or unknown meaning. Since it has not been possible to date the manuscripts of Lalla collections that Grierson and Barnett used, it has yet to be determined how long the transmission of her poetry was exclusively oral. The fact that Lalla's verses in old Kashmiri come to us in a modern form that is intelligible to any average Kashmiri speaker is an evidence in itself of oral transmission over a fairly long period of time. No doubt there were slow changes in the verses as the language changed. Kaul speculates that her verses over the centuries began to be sung by village minstrels and later became part of Kashmiri classical music (*sufiana kalam*) for they were now used as sacred invocations to open the assembly of sufis (*Majlis-e-marifin*). As time passed and the language slowly changed, some words in the original verses became unintelligible. These words were most probably replaced by new words so that the audience could understand the meaning of the obsolete words (Kaul 34). Even though the language of the verses changed slowly as the language changed, the thought content, images, and metaphors seems to have remained the same which gives the body of Lalla's compositions an inner coherence. As Grierson and Barnett rightly point out that "respect for the authoress and the metrical form of the songs have preserved a great many archaic forms of expression" (LV 7). It is for this reason the Grierson verse-collection based on two incomplete manuscripts as well as oral recension is more or less an accurate collection of the verses as scholars have maintained. However, becoming a part of the cultural repertoire also implies variants of the originals and creation of new verses modeled after the originals. Over the centuries, many such verses came to be associated with Lalla. From his extensive research of various Lalla collections, including verses cited in Persian sources, Jayalal Kaul concludes that 264 verses printed so far have been linked to Lalla. Though I agree with his general assertion that a great number of such printed verses are not in fact by her, I believe that his *Lal Ded* collection excludes many verses that could easily be attributed to the Lalla oeuvre.

Since Lalla's verses were orally transmitted for centuries, we can never be completely certain as to the authenticity of each and every verse. However, Lalla's unique use of images and metaphors, the specific content and style can be used as valid criteria for judging whether a particular verse can be attributed to her. The evocativeness of her verses arises from vivid and concrete images she used to convey her experiences. Some examples of her jewels: ***ami pana sodaras navi chyes laman*** (using untwisted yarn to pull a boat) or ***hachivi harinji petsiv kan*** (a grass arrow fitted on a wooden bow) for representing a weak will as she begins her quest, ***vuthan syeki lavar*** (twisting ropes of sand) for ineffectual efforts, ***amyen takyen poni zan shaman*** (water leaking from unbaked clay saucers) for unfocused attention, and ***manzabag bazaras kulfa rust van*** (shop without a lock in the midst of the market place) to represent her novice sense of self which has yet to develop powers of concentration and meditation to ward off outside temptations and exploitations.

The power of her verses can partly be attributed to this concrete and accessible style of image-making that impacts the listener. Common people could relate to these images and understand immediately what Lalla was attempting to convey, even when the concepts were highly esoteric. Each verse, consisting of four lines, usually stands as an independent unit, though there are a few written as question and answer—one verse stating the questions and the next the answers. Most of her verses, however, simply use vivid metaphors, without resorting to any explanations. It is left to the listener to make the connection and suggestively experience the import.

Lalla is truly an integral part of Kashmiri language,

literature and culture just as "Shakespeare is of English, Hafiz of Persian, and Kabir and Tulsidas [are] of Hindi" (Kachru 16). Kaul honours Lalla as the first modern Kashmiri poet and regards her as "the maker of *modern* Kashmiri language as well as literature" (Kaul 61). He attributes the linguistic and philological importance of Lalla's compositions in the history of Kashmiri language to the fact that these verses, even in the form they were narrated represented "a significant landmark in the linguistic transition from old to modern Kashmiri." He further notes that with "their many archaic expressions, forms and pronunciation notwithstanding, [they are] easy to understand and surprisingly modern, so that we may be justified in regarding them as the earliest specimen of modern Kashmiri" (Kaul 61). Some scholars have even written that her verses have made the Kashmiri language suitable for philosophical thought. All philosophical writing during her time was in Sanskrit, the language in which only the elite were proficient. In order to convey highly esoteric ideas to common people, she introduced terms and concepts originally absent in the Kashmiri language. The richness of her language, the turn of phrases, the metaphors that she uses have become standard expressions in modern Kashmiri. Her use of images is so specific to the context and culture of Kashmir that it has been difficult to produce a translation that has the beauty of the original.

As far as the translation of the verses is concerned, I agonized whether I should stick to the text of Lalla's verses or simply produce a free translation which is as poetic as the original. In order for Lalla's verses to have the same impact that it has in the original language, I would have had to find expressions and phrases from contemporary life that produced the same results, but then that would have meant producing a translation devoid of the spirit that I associate with Lalla's verses. As one fluent in both languages, Kashmiri and English, I feel the power as well as the poetry of Lalla's production, and am also acutely aware of the prosaic nature of my translation. Lalla is a treasured icon of Kashmiri culture, and it is fitting that her verses are translated both in their true spirit and as close to the original as possible.

CHAPTER TWO

Historical Background

In order to understand Lalla's life and her work, it is important that she be located within the historical moment she occupies. Female historiography has been problematic, especially when it concerns retrieving lives of women of the past historical periods. Kumkum Sangari argues that the historical reconstruction "hinges on understanding the particularly complex relation which obtains between social practices and representational forms. Since patriarchies function in and through relations of productions and divisions of labor as well as through diverse forms of discursivity, the material and discursive are mutually implicated—but there is no single relation between the two" (Sangari 1993, 871). For reconstructing Lalla's life, it is imperative that she be located within the historical moment she occupied while at the same time, it is necessary to explore the discursive representations of gender roles in broader religious and cultural narratives that guided the material existence of people during that period. It should also be noted that the formulations based on the Western feminist theory cannot be applied uncritically in this case as the social organization in medieval and pre-modern Europe was very different from that which prevailed in Kashmir in those times.

Kalhana's *Rajatarangini*, written in AD 1148–49, chronicles the history of Kashmir from the earliest times to AD 1150. Kalhana's primary focus is on the political history of Kashmir and his narrative centers around the succession of kings, political intrigues, invasions, and overthrows. Jonaraja continues Kalhana's chronicle beyond 1150 through 1450s which thus covers the period when Lalla lived. Jonaraja's *Rajatarangini*, too, focuses on the political history with very little to say about the social conditions in Kashmir during that time. However, it is clear from these narratives that the valley of Kashmir had to contend with competing kings and invaders for centuries. The later Hindu rule in Kashmir was filled with turbulence and ceaseless warfare, due to feuding within the valley and invasions from the outside. The society remained rigidly divided on the basis of caste and frequent invasions and mismanagement by the others left large sections in poverty. In the fourteenth century, the rulership of the kingdom of Kashmir finally passed from the hands of the Hindu kings into that of Muslim Sultans.

There are instances in medieval Kashmir when women played an important role in the affairs of the court. Queen Didda, Srilekha, Suryamati, Jayamati, and Kota Rani come to mind. Kota Rani in fact became the last Hindu ruler of Kashmir. She actively participated in running the administration for about three decades. During Sahadeva's rule (1301-20), Kota took an active role in helping the population when the tartar chief Dulchu invaded Kashmir and caused devastation and destruction before he left the valley. In this effort the fugitive Prince Rinchin aided her. When Rinchin became the new ruler, he married Kota. King Rinchin and Queen Kota worked together to administer the affairs of the state. Rinchin's rule lasted a short time as a rebellion resulted in his murder and the rulership was taken over in 1323 by Sahadeva's brother Udyanadeva. Kota married Udyanadeva and continued to be the real power behind the throne. Jonaraja describes her as "powerful; she was, as it were, the mind, and the king, the body, who carried out her orders" (JRT 24). When another tartar chief, Achala, invaded Kashmir, her husband fled leaving Kota behind to handle the crisis. Kota rose to the occasion and devised a clever diplomatic strategy that succeeded in bringing Achala's ruin. She continuously worked toward restoring prosperity in the valley. Jonaraja compares her to a canal that "nourishes cultivated fields with water," since she "nourish[ed] the people by bestowing much wealth on them" (JRT 30). On Udyanadeva's death in 1338 AD, she herself assumed the rulership which however lasted only for a few months because another aspirant to the throne, Shah Mir, planned a rebellion in which she was overthrown. Kota's overthrow marked the end of the Hindu rulership and the beginning of the Muslim rule.

Shah Mir ascended the throne in 1339 as Sultan Shams-ud-din and thus started the Sultan dynasty that ruled Kashmir for over two centuries. The early Sultans, Shams-ud-din (1339–1343), Ala-ud-din (1343–54), Shihab-ud-din (1354–73) and Qutb-ud-din (1373–89) were tolerant to non Islamic faiths and tried to bring an element of stability in the valley. Sultan Ala-ud-din worked hard to redress the suffering and destruction caused by the earlier invasion by Dulchu. Sultan Shihab-ud-din as a great administrator, builder, as well as a general, brought peace and stability within Kashmir and new conquests abroad (JRT 37–42). It is during the reign of Sultan Ala-ud-din, it seems that Lalla renounced her home and started the life of a wandering ascetic and she died when Shihab-ud-din ruled.

Going beyond conquests and defeats of kings and queens in the valley, there was also a cross-fertilization of ideas taking place continuously. Historical evidence indicates that, as a part of the Mauryan empire, Kashmir was introduced to Buddhism which, however, did not take firm roots till two centuries later. The Kushan king called Kanishka worked towards the spread of Buddhism in Kashmir and from there to Central Asia, China, Korea and Japan. However, with the decline of Kushans, the state patronage of Buddhism also declined. Shaivism was restored in the valley by the start of the sixth century by

Mihirbala, the king who took shelter in the valley on being defeated by the ruler of Malwa (Yashodhavarman) and by the king of Magadha (Baladitya). The spread of Islam in Central Asia brought yet another set of ideas into the Valley. While Mahmud of Ghazni with his attacks in 1015 left various places of worship in shambles, it was nearly 300 years later that Sayyid Bilal Shah, popularly called Bulbul Shah, worked for spreading Islam in Kashmir. Marco Polo mentions the presence of Islam in Kashmir in 1277 but it was during the reign of King Sahadeva that Bulbul Shah could spread his message of Islamic compassion and equality. This was further facilitated when Rinchin converted to Islam on becoming the king (to be called Sultan Sadruddin) and provided it with state patronage.

The initial spread of Islam in Kashmir was gradual as it was closely connected with the missionary activities of the Sufis from Persia and Central Asia who led simple and pious lives and mixed freely with the common people.[3] Their emphasis on social equality and their charitable acts made them highly respected amongst the common people who had suffered extensively due to general political intrigues as well as foreign invasions in the first half of the fourteenth century. As mentioned earlier the tartar chief Dulchu's invasion and his wanton plunder and destruction left the whole kingdom and its people devastated. Another invasion by Achala in the reign of Udyanadeva (1323–1338) was deflected by the political acumen of Queen Kota who practically ran the administration.

The Sufi teacher Mir Sayyid Ali, also known as Shah Hamadan, visited Kashmir three times, first in 1372 with an

[3] The school of Sufism developed when Islam came in contact with Hinduism and Buddhism in Central Asia and some parts of Persia. The fundamental beliefs of Sufism are very similar to esoteric Hinduism. The early Sufi missionaries in Kashmir were Sayyid Bilal Shah, Sayyid Jalal-ud-din, Sayyid Taj-ud-din, and most influential of all Sayyid Ali Hamadani (Shah Hamadan). See Bamzai 522–527.

entourage of 700 Sayyids, the second time in 1379, and a third time in 1384. He played an active role in converting the local population to the Islamic faith. The large scale adoption of Islam in the second half of the fourteenth century, Aurel Stein points out, "did neither affect the independence of the country nor at first materially change its political and cultural conditions. The administration remained as before in the hands of the traditional official class, the Brahmins,[4] for whom a change of religion presented no advantage and who accordingly retained their inherited status, together with its literary traditions" (130). Those who adopted Islam clung to traditional customs and beliefs so that there was little to distinguish them from those who did not change their religion. According to Hasan, the "Sultans of Kashmir, though of foreign origin, were not far behind their Muslim subjects in assimilating Hindu belief and usages. This was, of course, inevitable, for they lived surrounded by a population a majority of which was Hindu at least for a hundred years after the establishment of the Sultanate. Moreover, most of the Sultans had Hindu wives who, even after their conversion to Islam clung to their customs and who could not fail to influence their royal consorts and their children" (240). This peaceful co-existence did not last as towards the end of the fourteenth century, Sultan Sikandar (1389–1413) ascended the throne and became famous for religious bigotry. However,

[4] The word "brahmin" is used to refer to Hindus in general in Jonaraja's *Rajatarangini* that covers the period 1150–1459 AD which shows that the usage of "hindu" had not yet begun. Jonaraja's references to the persecution of Hindus is always in terms of the persecution of brahmins as if there was only one caste (JRT 59–75). The evidence does show that most of the lower caste Hindus had already converted to Islam by the end of the fourteenth century, so that there was mostly one caste (brahman) left in Kashmir. Also, since brahmins were the dominant caste, so the term was perhaps used to represent all Hindus around this time. The word "Hindu" and "Hindusthana" are found for the first time in Shrivara's *Jainarajatarangini* which covers the period 1459–1486 AD (Shrivara 161, 167).

religious tolerance was once again restored to the valley under the rulership of Sikandar's son Sultan Zain-ul-abdin (JRT 64–97) also popularly called Badshah (the generous king).

The predominant religion in Kashmir before Islam established itself was Shaivism which was ritualistic in nature. The monistic Shaivism, founded by Vasudeva in the ninth century, developed into a sophisticated philosophy, the Trika system, which was accessible to only a small population. Kalhana makes no reference to Abhinavagupta, the leading exponent of this system, though he does mention Shaiva cults who engaged in licentious acts in the name of tantric rituals (KRT 284–285). Even though Shaivism was the predominant religion in medieval Kashmir, Vaishnavism also flourished as is shown by temples and shrines of Vishnu built by various queens and kings. Sunil Chandra Roy notes that in Kashmiri Vaishnavism "we find a synthesis of the different Vaishnava cults which were current in ancient India. In it seems to have mingled the faith of the Vedic Vishnu, the system of Pancaratra school, the religion of the Satavata and the faith of the cowherd god Gopala Krishna. Rama was worshipped as an incarnation of Vishnu" (157). Because of the influence of Vaishnavism, both the *Mahabharata* and the *Ramayana* were popular in Lalla's time. Jonaraja's *Rajatarangini* refers to both the *Mahabharata* and the *Ramayana* as does Lalla in her verses (Verses 48, 96).

Exploring the reasons as to why Islam appealed to the common people of the fourteenth century Kashmir, P.N.K.Bamzai points out that with the disappearance of Buddhism, the predominant religion of Kashmir was Shaivism. It had ossified into a set of complicated rituals. In addition, all "the religious and philosophical books were in Sanskrit which, with the emergence of the popular Kashmiri language, became the domain of the privileged few, mostly of the Brahmin caste. Since the latter also carried on the civil administration, there grew up slowly a stiff though silent opposition to this class among the general mass of the people" (Bamzai 492). The religious and moral ferment was accompanied by political instability which led to changed social values that increased people's receptivity to the new faith.

The Sufi mystics lived pious and simple lives and engaged in compassionate acts to help the poor and the downtrodden. Legends speak of the Sufi and Hindu mystics gathering together frequently to exchange ideas and experiences. In fact Sheikh Nur-ud-Din (Nund Rishi), who was born toward the end of Lalla's life, is said to have had a high regard and reverence for Lalla. He started an order of Islamic Rishis in Kashmir which was founded on the ideals of love for all people irrespective of their caste, class, or religious creed. The order, open to both Muslims and Hindus saints and mystics, worked closely with the community, actively intervening on behalf of the people who were subject to injustices and oppression (Bamzai 469).

A legend describes Lalla's first meeting with Shah Hamadan in Khampor, a village situated ten miles to the southwest of Srinagar. Lalla encounters Shah Hamadan as she is sitting nude by the wayside; she wants to cover herself and thus runs into a grocery store, saying "I have seen a man". When the grocer turns her out, she runs into a baker's shop where the oven is red hot, ready for baking bread. Lalla jumps into the oven and emerges out dressed in golden clothes and hastens after Shah Hamadan (Koul 1921, 310). The legend is the basis of the proverb in Kashmiri: *ayeyi wanis gayi kandras*, (she came to the grocer, but instead went to the baker's). This hagiographic account is obviously meant to validate the spiritually advanced state of Shah Hamadan since he is the only 'real man' among the ordinary men she comes in contact with everyday. The legend also gives an interesting insight into gender issues. Lalla as a woman of flesh and bones is unfit to encounter such a man, and hence, she must go through the ordeal of fire to get rid of her physical impurities and emerge fully clothed before encountering the Sufi teacher.

Other legends, however, show Lalla's superiority to Sufi teachers. Lalla admonishes Shah Hamadan and Sheikh Nur-ud-Din (Nund Rishi) for showing off their occult powers by revealing her own which are far beyond theirs. Her critique of social and religious institutions of her time has led a few scholars to conclude that she adopted Sufi mysticism and brought about its synthesis with tantric Hinduism. G.M.D. Sufi states: "It is commonly avowed by Muslims in Kashmir that her verses after her contact with Shah Hamadan and other Muslim saints are more expressly reflective of Muslim thought" (385). As Jayalal Kaul argues, such an assumption is based on these scholars' unwillingness to seriously engage the esoteric tradition of Kashmiri Shaivism that permeates Lalla's verses. If Sufi mystics of Lalla's time seem to be speaking about similar experiences, it is because mystic traditions all over the world show some common features. No concrete evidence is available as to whether she even met Shah Hamadan and as for Sheikh Nur-ud-din; he was most probably too young to have influenced her (Kaul 72). If Lalla did indeed die at a fairly advanced age in the reign of Sultan Shihab-ud-din (1354–1373) and if Shah Hamadan first visited Kashmir in 1373, then there is no possibility of him influencing her. This, however, does not mean that other Sufis of the time did not have an influence on her thinking. Perhaps the free mingling of Sufi and Hindu mystics during this time resulted in their appreciation of genuine spiritual experience over religious dogmas of any kind. The Sufi mystics lived simple and devout lives and never abdicated their missionary spirit.[5] Lalla's verses also indicate that she

[5] In *Speaking of Siva*, A. K. Ramanujan writes that the 12th century medieval religious reform movement of Virashaivas, to which Mahadeviyakka belonged, arose out of the need for a living religion for the poor, the outcast, and the

followed an ascetic life style and sympathized with the plight of the common people. She advises them to live a life based on inner spirituality rather than outer religious dogma. Lalla's emphasis on religious and social equality as testified in her verses shows that she was secular in her outlook which is perhaps the reason why she has been held in such high reverence by Hindus and Muslims alike.

The political changes in the fourteenth century did not substantially change the political and administrative structure of the country, but the old elite began to lose its hegemony in the social arena. Initially Sanskrit remained the court language, however, it was increasingly mixed with Arabic and Persian words, until finally it was replaced by Persian. However, on the basis of the narrative evidence, it can be maintained that brahminical texts influenced gender-based and caste-based hierarchies and shaped the social relations. The position of women in the fourteenth century did not change drastically under the new rule. The upper class women continued to lead secluded lives whereas lower class women, especially in rural areas, went on working outdoors alongside their men in the

---

downtrodden who were outsiders to the established religion patronized by the rich. Virashaivas protested against the orthodox Hindu practices that privileged Brahmins who were mediators in any religious experience of members of other castes. Ramanujan notes that unlike Islam and Christianity the orthodox Hinduism is devoid of any missionary spirit. One is born a Hindu; one cannot become one. "With such a belief, there is no place for conversion in Hinduism; a man born to his caste or faith cannot choose and change nor can others change him. But if he believes in acquiring merit only by living and believing certain things, then there is room for choosing and changing his beliefs. He can then convert and be converted. If, as [Virashaiva] saints believed, he also believes that his god is the true god, the only true god, it becomes imperative to convert the misguided and bring light to the benighted. Missions are born. Bhakti religions proselytize, unlike classical Hinduism. Some of the incandescence of Virasaiva poetry is the white heat of truth seeking and truth-saying in a dark deluded world; their monotheism lashes out in an atmosphere of animism and polytheism" (Ramanujan 27).

field and the garden, as they did not have the luxury to stay indoors. The ruling class women were educated which is obvious from the fact that they opened schools, created endowments and built temples, mosques, or monasteries. Lower class women, however, were generally illiterate, though that might not have been the case for brahmin women as Lalla makes references to reading.

The patriachal control of the society was reinforced through epics like the *Mahabharata* and the *Ramayana*. These texts generally promote the patriarchal warrior ideology on the one hand and the ideal wifehood on the other. In the *Ramayana*, Sita is the ideal wife who accompanies her husband Rama into exile for fourteen years. During this time, she is abducted by the king of Lanka, Ravana, who holds her in captivity for some time while pressuring her to marry him. Sita refuses the offer and patiently waits for her husband Rama to save her from her plight. Rama defeats Ravana in a fierce battle and brings Sita back. However, since Sita has spent time under the protection of a man other than her husband, she must prove her purity by going through the ordeal of fire.[6] Her "self effacing nature, her steadfast loyalty to her husband, and her chastity make her both the ideal Hindu wife and the ideal *pativrata*. In a sense Sita has no independent existence, and no independent destiny. In all things she sees herself as inextricably bound up with Rama. Apart from him her life is meaningless" (Kinsley 76).

Aside from the epics, texts like the *Manavadharmashastra*

[6]When Rama returns to Ayodhya at the end of his exile, the people refuse to accept Sita as their queen because she had been under the protection of another man. Rama is forced to send her into exile where she gives birth to twin boys, Lava and Kusha. After several years have elapsed Rama, having overcome with guilt because of the injustice that he has meted out to his wife, sends for Sita under the condition that she prove her purity in a public ordeal. Sita returns and asks the earth to split open and accept her into her bosom into which she descends, never to return.

or the Laws of Manu lay down prescriptive rules for moral conduct in all aspects of life. In her analysis of Medhatithi's commentary on the *Manusmriti*, written in ninth century Kashmir, Kumkum Roy shows how it reinterprets the definition of the household (*grha*) in order to adapt it to the changed social situation that demanded including alternatives to the traditional norms. "It is evident," Roy notes, "that Medhatithi's definition of the *grha* was not identical with that of the *Manusmriti*. Although attempting to conform to the framework provided by the text, Medhatithi deviated in a number of respects—in conceding some degree of control over the resources of the household to kinswomen, in recognizing at least some space for procreative women, and in accepting the possibility of a less hierarchical relationship within the household" (13–14). While promoting some deviations from the norms, Medhatithi nonetheless accepts "the definition of marriage as an occasion for obtaining a wife for the patrilineal household. The woman thus obtained [is], moreover, ideally constructed as a subservient instrument for the maintenance and the perpetuation of the household and the patrilineage" (Roy 11). Medhatithi's commentary shows patriarchal power can work subtly through the modified social structures. The prescriptive norms might have been loosened and reinterpreted in medieval Kashmir as the society changed, but these reinterpretations nonetheless continued to be oppressive to women as these retained their grounding in hierarchical gender relations. Majority of women, either through internalization of values or through their external reinforcement, continued to lead lives that were determined by patriarchal social structures.

The authority of brahminical texts in medieval Kashmir, when brahmins controlled the religious, philosophical, and administrative apparatus, was most probably invoked frequently to maintain the caste status and to assure the purity of the progeny. The society was thus permeated with the ideology presented by Manu which has taken different forms in different historical periods depending on social and political forces shaping them. Whereas Manu's text can be briefly described as a long treatise on maintaining the privileged status of the priestly class, it also prescribes broad framework that should guide relationship between sexes within and outside the family. According to Manu "Men must make their women dependent day and night and keep under their own control those who are attached to sensory objects." Since women's innate nature (*strisvabhava*) is promiscuous, they must be constantly guarded so that they do not bring shame to the family. "Her father guards her in childhood, her husband guards her in youth, and her sons guard her in old age. A woman is not fit for independence" (Laws 197). Historically, this particular attitude towards women has guided the familial relations. It is even internalized by women to such an extent that they perceive their subservient and dependent status as natural which results in their own implication in perpetrating gender discrimination and oppression.

Indian texts, as Julia Leslie shows, describe two fundamental approaches toward women: one concerns the innate nature of women (*strisvabhava)* which is assumed to be wicked and the second is the self-effacing virtuous behavior of women (*stridharma)* and it is through the second that the first can be overcome. "The physical aspects of being female—menstruation, sexuality, childbirth, and so on—are taboo; women as biological creatures are condemned; the wild untamed goddesses, their counterparts in myth and symbol, are feared and appeased. Respect, even reverence, is reserved for those women in whom the biological has been controlled: the obedient wife, the selfless mother, and the gentle goddesses of the Indian imagination" (Leslie 7–8). Through engaging in virtuous behavior and exhibiting self-effacement and devotion to the family, women could, however, overcome their innate wickedness, so the texts say. Women's exploitation is thus perpetuated by these narratives, because good merits can be accumulated by them only if they follow the role prescribed for them. A selfless, devoted wife assures her place in the afterlife next to her husband. Women's lives thus shaped by the patriarchal ideology promotes passivity and self-effacement in women.

CHAPTER THREE

Lalla's Life

Lalleshwari was born into a brahmin family and her life was accordingly shaped by the familial relations prevalent in brahmin households of the fourteenth century Kashmir. Commenting on kinship structure amongst Kashmiri brahmins, T. N. Madan notes that in patrilinearly related households in a *kul* or clan "a woman's identity as wife overrides her other identities as daughter and sister and even as mother". Upbringing of girls takes place under the assumption that ultimately they are the property of in-laws which the parents are keeping in trust until the time of marriage. Madan adds that the wife serves the important function of the continuation of the patrilinear lineage. The importance of the wife's role in the kinship system is made clear by the status of a widow; widowhood changes a woman's status who is described as "a lost woman" and is not allowed to participate in rituals (205–206). Though a commentary on a more recent situation, Madan's words apply to Lalla's life as it is illustrated by the legends popular about her. Lalla was married at a young age and as she started her life with her husband's family, she was given a new name to mark her entry into her husband's family and her break from her natal family. As a married woman, she lived in a joint family where the mother-in-law ran the household and made her life miserable. Her mother-in-law's tyrannical behavior toward her is the subject of several legends. None of the legends have anything to say about her natal family which points to the fact that she probably had minimal connection with them after her marriage.

The tyrant mother-in-law stories so common in India can be explained in terms of women's confinement to the private sphere where they establish alternative power centers indirectly based upon and enforced by patriarchal power—very often leading to the perpetuation of their own or of other women's oppression within the family (Sangari 1993, 871). In order to explain the complex hierarchical relations that emerge as the patriarchal arrangements affect the working of the family, Sangari points out that it is too simplistic to portray women as victims of these arrangements as these are directly related to other sources of social inequality based on caste or class. The political structures along with cultural and religious practices serve to create material conditions as well as ideology of society, so that women themselves become complicit in their own oppression as well as those of other men and women of lower castes. Sangari finally concludes that "women's implication in the contractual and consensual elements of a patriarchy not only puts them in a contradictory relation with the patriarchy itself, but also tends to situate their social agency in fairly contradictory fashion as both complicit and transgressive" (869). The contradictory position that women occupy in their complicity in as well as transgression of patriarchal arrangements makes any analysis of female subjectivity and cultural productions by women a much more complex affair. In recovering women's lives finally, it is the gaps and absences that are often more revealing than what is recorded about them in the chronicles or official histories. Scholars who have worked on Lalla thrive on showing the continuity between her life and work, but my project is to focus on discontinuities and contradictions of her life. Discrepancies are typically glossed over by interpretations which ignore the role that gender plays in shaping subjectivity.

An effective feminist analysis of Lalla's life should resist seeing it arranged along a unified linear axis, since as a woman in a stratified society, her subjectivity occupied many axes of power at the same time. The privileges along one axis were counterbalanced by oppression along some other axes. As a brahmin woman, she had access to home-based education unlike her lower caste sisters but she was more constrained by the ideology of the ideal chaste brahminical wife who had to guard her sexuality as well as any future progeny. Finally, as a woman in a patriarchal society she was affected by the subordinate position in her own family and in society at large. Lalla's life then must be seen as occupying multiple subject positions in a web of relations determined by her gender, caste, and class. In the medieval times, ties of kinship and family were of paramount importance since people defined themselves more through their collective identity with the family than their individual identity. As a part of the feudal society, Lalla was caught at the crossroads between its gender-based social limitations and her individual beliefs—an added burden to any woman's emancipatory journey. In order to find a space for herself that was not circumscribed by patriarchal ideology, she was compelled to make a break with the social as well as family relations. As she disengaged herself from the socially constructed gender roles, she had to articulate and define a new space for herself, without any support from the community. Lalla's journey was a solitary one where she fumbled and struggled as she uncovered inch by inch another mode of existence that was outside the patriarchal social and religious arrangements at one level, but intimately tied to it at another.

We have only orally transmitted legends about Lalla who has been a part of the daily repertoire in most Kashmiri households for centuries. Jonaraja's *Rajastarangini* which covers the period when Lalla lived does not mention her at all. Scholars have wondered why in spite of being such an integral part of Kashmiri language and culture she was left out of the Sanskrit literature of the following centuries. One of the reasons for this neglect could have been that the chronicles focused mainly on kings and the political intrigues surrounding them. It has also been speculated that she has been absent from the chronicles because she rejected conventional morality and social norms; "she did not observe the formalities of ceremonial piety; she was vehemently critical of orthodoxy, its dogma and ritual, its hypocrisy and exclusiveness; and (what they would certainly not approve of) she spoke of the secret doctrine and its disciplines to all" (Kaul 3). She lived in the countryside and it was the common people who treasured her verses. This made her a part of the popular Kashmiri folk imagination rather than the elite brahminical tradition. Kaul notes that the earliest reference to Lalla is in Baba Dawud Mishkati in his *Asrar-ul-Abrar* (The secrets of the Pious), a hagiographic document written in 1654. Mishkati describes her as Lalla Arifa, an advanced mystic, and relates the water pitcher legend about her (1–2). The first Persian chronicle to mention her name is Muhammad Azam Dedamari's *Waqi 'ati Kashmir* that was completed in 1746. The two other Persian chronicles *Tarikhi-Hasan* (1835) and *Tarikhi-Kabir* (1909–10) also make references to her (Kaul 1–5).

Lalla was born in the beginning of the fourteenth century. A great deal of controversy exists as to when exactly she was born. Anand Koul who published a collection of seventy five Lalla's verses in *Indian Antiquary* in 1930s, gives the date of her birth, without citing his sources, as the middle of the fourteenth century and the place of her birth as Pandrenthan which was four miles to the south east of Srinagar (Koul 1921, 302). Kaul's study of Persian sources shows, however, that Lalla in fact was born somewhere between 1317 and 1320, even as early as 1300–1301. This would explain the time frame in the first reference to Lalla in *Waqi' ati Kashmir* (1746) which describes her having flourished or become famous during the reign of Sultan Alau-ud-Din (1344–55) and having died during the reign of Sultan Shihab-ud-din (1353–73). Kaul argues that the term *Zahurash namud* in Persian means both "was born" and "became known" and has been misinterpreted by authors of later chronicles who took the period when she became famous as the period when she was born. If we accept Dedamari's time period as the time when she became famous (the water pitcher incident marking the time of her renunciation), then the later date of her birth would make her about twelve years old at the time of her renunciation. This does not match the evidence we have from other legends which tell us about her long unhappy married life (Kaul 4–6).

Lalla was educated at home as was customary those days in most brahmin families. She was given in marriage to Nicha Bat of Pampore at a young age where she received a new name Padmavati. The custom of giving a new name to a bride as she is accepted into her husband's family still exists in Kashmir. It symbolizes a married woman's new identity as the wife and the daughter-in-law. In this capacity she must disconnect herself from her natal family and devote her services to her marital family. Lalla, however, always refers to herself by her maiden name and it is this name that has come down to posterity.

Legends speak about her mother-in-law as a tyrant who filled her married life with suffering. Lalla was not given enough to eat. Her mother-in-law would serve her a small portion of rice which was made to look larger as it had a stone hidden underneath. She would quietly eat whatever she was served without protest. Once a special *grahashanti* ceremony was held at her house. As she went out that day to fetch water from the river, one of her neighbors teased her that she would have a feast that night. Lalla's reply has become a famous proverb in Kashmiri as "*hund maritan kinah kath noshi nalvat tsalih nah zanh*" which means whether a lamb or a sheep is killed at her house, the daughter-in-law will always get scraps (Koul 1921, 303). Narratives showing her as a victim of women's oppression want to present Lalla as a woman who would have been a good wife if she had not been ill-treated by her mother-in-law.

Some legends describe her marriage not being consummated, while others say she was a disobliging wife who preferred to keep to herself. All legends agree that she was introspective and did not show a great deal of interest in worldly affairs. The famous water pitcher legend describes the incident that finally sets her on the path of renunciation. According to the legend, Lalla got up before dawn every day and walked to the river bank in Zinpura village to fetch water in a pitcher. She crossed the river to visit the shrine of Natta Keshava Bhairava by the river bank and spent a prolonged period of time there before returning home with a pitcher of water on her head. Her husband started suspecting her of infidelity and one day followed her to the river bank where he found her sitting alone in a meditative posture. He went home without saying anything and waited for her to come back. Soon Lalla returned with an earthen pitcher full of water on her head. Filled with rage, her husband hit the pitcher with his stick; the pitcher broke into pieces, but the water stayed miraculously intact on her head. Lalla calmly went inside the house, and poured the water into smaller vessels until all vessels were full. She took the left-over water and threw it outside where a pond was formed. Later on, this pond was named *Laltrag* (the Pond of Lalla) which is said to have been full of water for many centuries.

Legends are hagiographic accounts created by later generations who embellish historical facts by giving them a sacred turn to make them appear miraculous. Instead of taking them as literal truths, a deeper meaning could be gleaned from them if we read them for what they do not say. If we shift our gaze to the stick that crashed the pitcher into pieces, instead of focussing on the shining water, shaped like a pitcher, on top of Lalla's head, it is equally meaningful to say, that this incident represented a turning point in Lalla's life because she had enough of this cruel treatment at home, from the hands of her husband as well as her mother-in-law. The violence exhibited by her husband, may have been the crucial incident which made her reject her family altogether.

The Lalla of legend comes across as a gentle, suffering wife who does not in any active way try to stop the ill-treatment handed out to her. Instead, she withdraws into her own space and seeks refuge in spiritual practices as the only sphere where she could have control over her life. Lalla's renunciation of home and family, one can speculate, was the result of her dissatisfaction with traditional gender roles as she had no recourse to socially accepted ways to express her difference from the flock. Some of Lalla's verses illustrate her struggle to find the right path for herself as she renounces the protection of her home and family.

The need to develop concentration and will power to transcend the physical and the social constraints allows her to explore her subjectivity along a different axis not directly affected by patriarchal institutions or traditional gender definitions. As she starts on her journey, she is told by her teacher to be detached, but she finds it very hard to achieve detachment. The whole process of proceeding on her chosen path becomes painful to her. She breaks the bonds that connect her to her friends and family. In this state, she compares her body to an unlocked shop in the midst of the market place. She finds herself vulnerable to attacks from the outside—not only in the form of exploitation, but also temptations.

Historically, women have seldom been the desiring subjects but merely the objects of desire, reinforcing the role of socially conditioned passivity and self-abnegation. Lalla who rejects passivity and self-abnegation must feel her position as a desiring subject even more acutely. She must continuously remind herself of the transitoriness of worldly things. In one of her verses, she says:

> I will gently lament for you
> O mind, you are in love with illusions
> Not a shadow of this worldly splendor will accompany you
> Oh, why do you forget your real nature (V 7)

In yet another verse, she describes her own desires as a candy load on her shoulders which she experiences as a burden because they bind her to worldly things.

> Loosened is the shoulder knot of my candy load
> Bent like a bow is my body
> How can I carry this burden?
> My guru's words to achieve detachment are painful
> Like a flock without a shepherd am I
> How can I carry this burden? (V 4)

Lalla depicts the world in which she has a gendered existence in terms of a river which she must cross in order to reach the other world where her fulfillment lies. Both the boat, which is the body, and the river, which is the world, are only important in so far as they provide a medium in which to live out one's bodily existence. Another metaphor she uses for her body is "royal castle" and her subjectivity as an "unskilled carpenter". So the "carpenter" must develop power to act upon the body to control and transcend its desires. Even while at one level, there is a need to transcend dualism, at another level her words are marked by a dualism of mind and body, where the former is privileged and the latter presented as a solid opaque matter to be worked on and even discarded. The ultimate quest, then, for Lalla is to transcend her embodied existence, even as it is her embodied self that enables her to seek transcendence. In one of her verses, she says:

> Impurities of the heart I burned
> Desires I killed

> Lalla, my name, shone only
> When I surrendered completely (V18)

There is nothing unusual about Lalla's insistence on cultivating detachment as all religious traditions regard it necessary to cultivate the awareness of the ephemeral nature of worldly things in order to seriously pursue the path of knowledge. However, Kashmir Shaivites also believe that once the enlightened perspective is achieved the material reality can be enjoyed for what it is—the play of consciousness. In spite of that, most of Lalla's verses point only in the direction of transcendence.

By focusing on transcendence, Lalla follows the patriarchal discourse, casting the world in a conflictual stance, wherein the self must transcend the other. On the metaphysical level, this conflict is resolved by transcendence of the physical, whereas on the physical level, the male self posits women and subaltern groups as the other which must be transcended as the self moves toward higher unity. The male-centered notion of subjectivity which Lalla exemplifies is based on setting the other as the opposite against which the self has to guard itself so that it does not crack the brittle boundaries in which it finds itself enclosed.

One might wonder at this point to what extent are the contemporary western sociological analyses of gender relations valid for the medieval society in Kashmir that was defined primarily through feudal modes of production as well as consumption. If we look at the medieval Kashmiri society only in terms of the means of production and consumption, then the application of the present analyses might not be valid. But the feudal Kashmiri society was also determined to a great extent by various brahminical discourses which in some ways transcend historical specificities, even as they are determined by the broader historical situation. The Hindu metaphysics of transcendence is based on the othering of the world which is reduced to an illusion that must be transcended in order to attain enlightenment. My use of western theorists is then only as a heuristic device to study the shaping of subjectivity in broadest possible terms in so far as it manifests itself in naturalized gender roles, the woman given the role of nurturing and relating and the men that of autonomy and agency.

In a sociological analysis of these two modes of experience within patriarchal culture, Nancy Chodorow draws on psychoanalytic theories of male and female personality development and demonstrates that traits of nurturing and relatedness are not biologically determined or even a result of conscious role training. Instead they are very much built into the structure of the family and society that reproduces the gender roles and sexual division of labor. "Women, as mothers, produce daughters with mothering capacities and the desire to mother. These capacities and needs are built into and grow out of the mother-daughter relationship itself. By contrast, women as mothers (and men as not-mothers) produce sons whose nurturant capacities and needs have been systematically curtailed and repressed. This prepares men for their less affective later family role, and for primary participation in the impersonal extrafamilial world of work and public life" (Chodorow 7). Relatedness taken to an extreme can lead to the dispersion of self while extreme individualization can lead to disconnection from the other. The discourse that revolves around the need for detachment from the world tends to give rise to constructions of the self that favor individualization over relatedness even in medieval Kashmir where one's identity was more defined in collective rather than individual terms.

Lalla's life shows a schism between the two moments of individualization and relatedness because of her contradictory location. The separation that Lalla sees between her social self and her "real self" already divides reality into two compartments, the socially interrelated self and the Self that transcends these relations. The ideology which underestimates the importance of material life and promotes narratives of the spiritual journey as a return home ignores the issues of caste, class, and gender that shape women's material existence. This attitude affects women negatively since it encourages the acceptance of social injustices and thereby perpetuates oppressive power structures.[7] However, even within this framework, Lalla manages to be subversive as in a number of her verses she speaks about creating a third space that goes beyond the binary dualities—this world/other world, Shiva/Shakti, even male/female.

The idea of self-containment is intrinsic to Hindu worldview as revealed in myths as well as in the Kashmiri Shaiva texts. The latter, however, have potential to be interpreted in ways that could be emancipatory for women. To say that Lalla actually read the Shaiva texts would be to plunge into ahistoricism and deny her the specificity of the historical moment she occupies. Her worldview is very much shaped by the ideology of the medieval period. In spite of remarkable insights into the nature of reality she attains through her Shaivite practice, she can only experience these insights in a disembodied fashion, without integrating them into her lived reality. This in fact limits her potential to lead a fulfilling life at the physical level, even as she achieves an advanced state of awareness at the spiritual level.

Some verses express her vulnerability, her sense of being overwhelmed in the face of her rejection of the protection provided by her family and of finding herself in a space without role models. The only model of social self available to her under the circumstances is that of the highly individuated self which thrives on disconnection and self-containment rather than

[7]As Mary Daly has shown, the motif of circular journey, exit and return or alienation and reunion, is a common occurrence in the western traditions, too, and has in fact been a source of oppression for women because by focusing on the other world, the social injustices of this world are easily ignored (23).

social relatedness. Lalla describes her journey in this unexplored territory as perilous and she feels the need to train her mind as well as body in order to survive. This world where she has rejected all social bonds now becomes a temporary residence; her real home lies in the other world which is free of spatio-temporal dimensions and hence, of lived social reality. In order to develop this type of self-contained subjectivity, Lalla exercises rigorous self-discipline which involves clearing her mind of desires because these would otherwise bind her to the world of transitory things. The solitariness of her new life is expressed in the following verse:

> Arduous was my search for the Self
> Nothing compares to the hidden knowledge
> Self-absorption led me to the house of nectar
> Cups I found filled to the brim but nobody was drinking (V 17)

Lalla is thus aware of her isolation not only in the secular world which she has renounced, but also in the spiritual world where she is an outsider to the written Kashmiri Shaiva tradition. She has no way to share her experiences with those who could understand her. She also does not have access to the experiences of women, oral or written, that preceded her. In contrast to Lalla, the seventeenth century mystic poet Rupa Bhavani specifically mentions the sustenance that she derived from Lalla's life and her verses. Even though Rupa finds Lalla's life continuing in her own, she does not feel the need to reject her family and community by turning herself into a wandering ascetic. In spite of leaving home for brief periods of time, Rupa nonetheless remained integrally connected to her family and community.

Lalla's refusal to perform female gender is illustrated by the legends that describe her roaming in a nude state after she renounces her family. Such legends are based on the following verse:

> My guru gave me only one advice—
> From outside transfer the attention within
> That became my initiation
> That is why I began to wander naked (V 15)

The Kashmiri word *natsun* can be translated as both "to dance" and "to wander". Some scholars have literally interpreted the last line as pointing to her practice of dancing naked in a God-intoxicated state (LV107). Others have gone so far as to state that just before she started Shaiva practice she developed a big belly (*lol*) which covered her private parts (Koul 1921, 304). Still others have chosen to see *nangay* as a transformation of *nonga* (name of a mountain flower) and hence, translated *nangay natsun* as "dancing like a mountain flower" (KS 5). Aside from the concrete fact that freezing Kashmiri winters are hardly conducive to wandering in a nude state, my own interpretation of this verse is based on considering it within the context of her other verses. Lalla's wandering in a nude state could refer to her divesting or derobing herself of all worldly attachments, including her family, friends, and the comfort of a home. It could also point to her refusal to perform her gender in that she pays no attention to traditional feminine modes of dress or behavior. This approach is in line with the interpretation of her other verses which use a great many analogies and metaphors to convey highly esoteric ideas and experiences. If the underlying thought system within which Lalla elaborates her experiences were not known, the literal translation of her verses or her legends would fail to explain why Lalla had such a deep impact on the common people who have ultimately been responsible for keeping the words and fragments of her life alive for us for so many centuries.

As Lalla rejects social conventions, she is subject to ridicule which causes a great deal of pain to her. At the same time, it makes her focus even more intensely on her practice, now that she occupies a space outside the system. She says in a verse:

The chain of embarrassment will only break
When I can tolerate taunts and mocking words
Robe of self-pity will burn away
When the inner unbridled horse is brought under control (V 23)

Lalla's refusal to conform is not taken to kindly by community members. They gossip about her scandalous lifestyle. She endures the gossip by ignoring it and by staying focused on her goal. Thus, she says:

I endured verbal abuse as well as slander
Scandals broke out about my past and present
I am Lalla and my yearning never stopped
When I achieved my goal, nothing affected me (V 25)

Lalla develops a thick skin for insults and abuses that are hurled at her and she learns not to lose her equanimity. A story about her relates how street urchins would sometimes hurl insults at her. Once a kindhearted shopkeeper, a cloth merchant, scolds the young urchins for their behavior and sends them away. However, Lalla calmly asks him for a long piece of cloth which she tells him to cut into two equal parts and to weigh them separately. Then she drapes one piece on her left shoulder and the second on her right shoulder. She ties a knot in the piece on her right shoulder when someone calls her a bad name and ties a knot in the other piece as she is shown respect by somebody else. In the evening she brings back the two pieces of cloth to the shopkeeper and asks him to weigh them once again—both pieces weigh exactly as they had before (Koul 1921, 306).

Lalla's response reveals her belief in herself, her self-reliance, and her commitment to the new direction she has taken in her life despite what people say about her. The above legend also indicates how resistance to patriarchal norms has not been easy for women even when they have devoted themselves to spiritual disciplines. As a result women who have rejected traditional gender definitions, have felt the need to follow the model of a self-contained self, in order to survive the hostile social environments. Without any social support this would have been their last refuge in establishing and maintaining a new identity outside the patriarchally ordered relations. Some of her verses deal with this issue:

> Let them hurl abuses at me or lecture me
> Let them call me what they wish
> Let them offer me flowers of devotion
> I am untouched, so what will they gain by it (V 66)
>
> Even if thousands of abuses are hurled at me
> In my heart I am not hurt
> If I am a devotee of all-pervading Shiva
> Ashes cannot soil the mirror (V 77)

After Lalla renounces her family, she spends the rest of her life as a wandering ascetic without any fixed home. Kashmir has a long history of asceticism which is usually contrasted with the householder's life—the two occupying different locations, the former a forest hermit and the latter a family person. Patrick Olivelle argues that these were the society's ideal types, in fact, the Indian ascetic traditions "were never totally asocial or antisocial." The "rhetoric, images, and rituals tended to accentuate their separation from familial and social life." However, he adds, 'domestication' was "the process whereby that rhetoric and those images and rituals were transformed to reflect the absorption of asceticism at least partially into the life of society" (12–13). Lalla's break with family and kinship ties and her refusal to participate in economic, ritual, and social activities, therefore, do not signify her becoming asocial or antisocial. She still retains a partial bond with society as her verses testify though only as a social critic and teacher.

Lalla seems to have an awareness of the social construction of gender roles at some level. In one of her verses, she says she came to the world like a blooming cotton flower with all the potential and possibilities intact, full of enthusiasm and aspiration. However, the ginner and the carder of society reduced her to a miserable state and turned her into utility-full fine yarn which is hung on the weaver's loom to be turned into cloth. Her social self is the creation of others to be used by others. She compares overcoming the conditioning to the washerman washing a piece of cloth thoroughly and rubbing it with soap and washing soda (a cleansing agent). The washed clean piece of cloth is cut by the tailor into bits; Lalla the daughter, Lalla the daughter-in-law, and Lalla the wife are simply torn into shreds and her true identity emerges. Both washerman and tailor in this verse are Shiva or the Self within herself, the realization of which finally helps her overcome the patriarchally defined "feminine" self which she experiences as oppressive:

> I, Lalla, set out in the hope of blooming like a cotton flower
> Ginner and carder gave me hard blows
> The female spinner spun me into fine yarn
> In the weaver's shop I was stretched on the loom (V 13)
>
> The washerman then dashed me on a slab of stone
> Rubbing me with much soap and washing soda
> Then the tailor cut me into bits with scissors
> And only then I, Lalla, attained supreme bliss (V 14)

Lalla uses the female gender for the spinner which refers to women who are traditionally regarded as the bearers of culture and the reproducers of gender roles in the next generation. The washerman and the tailor, both of male gender, are Lalla's liberators whose deliberate actions lead to the disintegration of the socially constructed gendered self and to the emergence of her true identity. The use of male liberators, though used metaphorically, reflects Lalla's unawareness of the subtleties through which the patriarchal power structure works to keep women from forming a sense of community with other women who can contribute toward their emancipation. The transcendental reality which is characterized by gender-neutrality and universality has attributes that are traditionally associated with the masculine. At the popular imaginative level, these attributes are translated into the masculine or the male deity as the prime figure in women's spiritual salvation, which in turn causes the repetition of the hierarchical gendered relationship in women's religious experience.

If we compare Lalla to another medieval poet/singer Mirabai (b. 1498), it is obvious that Lalla is more radical and challenges the patriarchal social norms at a deeper level. In a detailed analysis of Mira's songs that belong to the *bhakti* tradition, Kumkum Sangari notes the abundance of images of subordination, subalternity, and bondage. The *Vishnu Purana*, the *Bhagavad Gita*, and the *Bhagavat Purana* include women and *shudras* (low-caste people) "as listeners to the stories and teachings of the epics and Puranas. Here, simultaneous with the description of the subjection of women and s[h]udras and of their essential 'fallen' nature, there occurs, inversely, a metaphorical enrichment and idealization of subalternity" (1990, 1471).

In high brahminical tradition, the brahmins are intermediaries between this world and God, but the *bhakti* tradition circumvents that by making it possible for the lower caste people and women to directly commune with God by simply showing devotion to Krishna, the cowherd-prince. Krishna in his dual role is both a subaltern, constantly performing actions that go against social norms, and a prince who acts as the ideal ruler devoted to his hundreds of wives. Mira, a Rajput princess, renounces home and family and devotes her life to Krishna. She associates with people from lower castes and expresses her devotion to Krishna through singing and dancing. Sangari argues convincingly that even though Mira challenges patriarchal institutions and gender roles at one level, she recreates and relives the very relations and hierarchical dualities in the spiritual realm. Mira's songs are filled with desire for Krishna, but this desire is ultimately only imaginary, because it can not be fulfilled on the physical plane. She uses the language of subalternity and subordination to describe her relationship to Krishna. She regards herself as his servant, his wife, and his lover. Her attitude to him is more like a courtesan than that of a moral wife.[8]

As reflected in their compositions, Mira and Lạlla embody very different types of female subjectivity. Whereas Mira challenges patriarchal social institutions at one level, she reproduces the underlying oppressive gender relations at another level. Lalla, on the other hand, resists the female gendered self both in the secular as well as spiritual realm. Mira remains a sexualized female even after her renunciation, whereas Lalla adheres to the male-defined self in her rejection of traditionally defined attributes of feminine self-effacement, that are often accompanied by devotional and supplicant approach toward spiritual experience. She takes control of her experience as a self-contained subjectivity, identifying more with Shiva than with Shakti. This approach is associated with extreme austerities, self-containment, and self-absorption. Lalla challenges the patriarchal institutions by renouncing her husband and her family. She also critiques the religious institutions and practices of her time. Because of occupying multiple subject positions, that of a woman, an upper caste woman, who chooses to follow spiritual practices traditionally available only to men, she sees through the facade of prescriptive religious ideology which perpetuates gender and caste hierarchy. Her verses are devoid of the devotional and self-effacing language that is so typical of Mira's songs. Many of her verses do not depict Shiva as a male deity, instead Shiva is described as the transcendental reality

[8]My discussion of Mirabai is based on Kumkum Sangari's article "Mirabai and the Spiritual Economy of *Bhakti*" in *Economic and Political Weekly*, July 7, 1990.

that is the ground of empirical reality. Lalla thus resists patriarchal construction of female gender.

Lalla's life can also be compared to the medieval Shaiva mystic poet Mahadeviyakka who lived in Karnataka in the12th century. She is known to have defied social rules and customs, thrown away modesty and wandered in a nude state, her body covered with her long hair. Mahadevi's poetry (*vachanas*) spoken in Kannada show a curious blend of bhakti tradition and Shaiva monotheism. In these, she expresses her love and devotion to Cenna Mallikarjuna, a form of Shiva. She describes him as her husband, lover, and father. The only aspiration of her life is to be united with him.

Some accounts say that Mahadeviyakka's youth and beauty impressed the feudal lord so much that he made her his wife. Other accounts insist that she did not marry anybody. In any case, Mahadevi's poetry shows that she did not want to have anything to do with husbands of flesh and blood. She says defiantly, "Take these husbands who die, decay, and feed them to your kitchen fires!"[9] Her use of the genre of love poetry to articulate her spiritual experience seems to have historical reasons as women in medieval times were either seen as or saw themselves as a wife,a mother or a lover. In fact when Mahadevi visits the school of Virashaiva mystics, founded by Basavanna in Kalyana, she engages in a verbal exchange with the head of the assembly, Allama Prabhu, who tests her to see if she is worthy to join the fellowship. The first question that she is asked is to identify her husband if she wants to stay. Mahadevi tells them that she is married to Cenna Mallikarjuna. The verbal exchange that ensues soon after convinces the assembly of her advanced spiritual state and she is accepted into the circle. In some of her poems, Mahadevi describes her initiation into the fellowship in

[9] Mahadeviyakka. *Speaking of Siva*, p. 142.

terms of a marriage ritual when she becomes Cenna Mallikarjuna's wife:[10]

> Setting a canopy of fire
> Over an altar made of water,
> Spreading a hailstone carpet,
> He came and wedded
> A headless bridegroom to a legless bride.
> They gave me to a life never to be shaken off!
> They married me to a groom
> Named Cenna Mallikarjuna[11]

In yet another poem when she attains self realization, she says:

> After my body became
> Thyself, whom could I serve?
> After my mind became
> Thyself, whom could I invoke?
> After my breath became
> Thyself, whom could I worship, pray?
> After my consciousness was lost in Thee,
> Whom could I know?
> Being Thyself in Thee,
> Cenna Mallikarjuna Lord,
> Through Thee have I forgotten Thee![12]

Mahadeviyakka's aim, as reflected in her poetry, is to achieve a mystic union with Shiva which transcends all subject/object duality. She belonged to the Virashaiva religious reform movement of mystics who rejected caste and class hierarchy and protested against ritualistic and orthodox Shaiva religion which focused around complex daily rituals. The South Indian Shaiva religion, based on the *Shaivasiddhanta*, is essentially dualistic in nature, dividing reality into Shiva (*pati*), the fet-

[10] For a detailed account of this exchange, see Swamy's *The Virasaiva Saints: A Study*, pp 98–102.

[11] Mahadeviyakka. Quoted in Swamy's *The Virasaiva Saints*, p. 104.

[12] Mahadeviyakka. Quoted in Swamy's *The Virasaiva Saints*, pp. 104–105.

tered soul (*pashu*), and factors that bind it (*pasha*). Shiva creates the world to allow the fettered soul to liberate itself. However, liberation does not imply that the individual is united with Shiva, instead the two remain eternally separate. Virashaiva reformers, on the other hand, absorbed the monotheistic elements of Hinduism and bridged the eternal gulf between the individual and Shiva by asserting that it was indeed possible for the individual to be reunited with Shiva. Thus, Shiva and the individual (*jiva*) did not belong to two different orders of reality, but one was infolded in the other. Virashaivas also protested against the complex rituals that could only be performed by brahmins who thus became intermediaries in the religious experience of the common people. Virashaivas proclaimed, no external worship of any kind was required for spiritual experience. It was indeed possible for all individuals, irrespective of caste, creed, gender, or occupation, to directly experience Shiva. Shiva's evolution into Many, they propounded, takes place through his power Shakti and the return from the Many to the One results from his power Bhakti.[13] So Shakti and Bhakti go together in Virashaiva worldview which explains the bhakti orientation of Mahadevi's poetry. Virashaiva mystics, like Lalla, were great synthesizers in that they brought highly esoteric ideas to common people and thus joined the high brahminical tradition and the folk traditions of their time, often using Sanskrit words or images along with folk imagery in poetry uttered in Kannada.[14]

[13] For an extended discussion of Virsashaiva thought, see Swamy's *The Virasaiva Saints: A Study*.

[14] According to Ramanujan, Virashaivas reject external worship of all kinds. *Jangama* or the religious mendicant is central to their practice, as the external temple worship is replaced by worshipping the body as the temple. The Virashaiva trinity is the guru, the *linga*, and the *jangama*. Virashaivas were wandering ascetics who went from place to place spreading their message to the people that there is only one God and that is Shiva. Their religious lyrics

Mahadeviyakka's poetry is similar to Mira in its bhakti orientation, even as it is closer to Lalla's in its philosophical and esoteric content. Unlike Lalla, Mahadevi makes aesthetic dimension central to her spiritual quest which is reflected in the signature line in all her poems which makes a reference to Cenna Mallikarjuna, (translated both as "lovely Arjuna Lord of goddess Mallika" or "lovely lord, white as jasmine"). The literal translation suggests both the aroma as well as the beauty of jasmine flowers whereas the qualifier "white" represents her quest to be united with a state that is devoid of all distinctions. Some of her poems resemble the romantic nature poetry of the West. Due to the double meaning, Mahadevi's poetry could be interpreted by listeners according to the level of their spiritual progress. Mahadevi died at a young age, in her twenties, yet her lyrics continue to dazzle people even now. Both Mahadevi's and Lalla's words reveal their knowledge of the esoteric aspects of Shaivism. Mahadevi makes human love a metaphor to represent her mystic experience as her path is that of devotion. One could perhaps say that what Mahadeviyakka acquired through intense *bhaktiyoga*, Lalla achieved through concentrated *jnanayoga*. The path they adopted were different, even as it seems their aim was the same.

Lalla's verses reveal her deep knowledge of the esoteric practices of Kashmiri Shaivism which were traditionally part of the secret tradition. She was initiated into Shaiva yoga by

---

(*vachanas*) are an outpouring of subjective experience. Ramanujan contrasts the Virashaiva poetry with the traditional *shruti* (to be heard) and *smriti* (to be remembered) literature in that it is an outpouring of the heart and is a description of unmediated experience. Thus, for Virashaivas the spiritual experience is "a search for the 'unmediated vision', the unconditioned act, the unpredictable experience. Living in history, time and cliché, one lives in a world of the pre-established, through the received (*sruti*) and the remembered (*smriti*). But the Experience when it comes, comes like a storm to all such husks and labels" (Ramanujan 31).

Siddha Shri Kanth and through her sincere hard practice, it is said, she soon surpassed even her teacher. Since the teachings were imparted only to a select few, Lalla was the first woman we know of who openly spoke about these practices to common people. Her oral transmission can be seen as a subversive act to resist the written discourse to which she and other people did not have access. In one of her verses she says that she learned some things from books, but others she learned through direct experience. Thus, she emphasizes direct experience more than any elaborate study of texts.

> What I read, I followed, the unreadable I got through direct experience
> I brought down the lion from the forest like a jackal
> My teachings for others, I followed myself
> Only then I attained knowledge and achieved my goal[15] (V 53)

Her life in many ways represents a challenge to the prescriptive ideology of brahminical texts, including the *Gita* which stresses the importance of duty in the interaction with others. Krishna advises Arjuna to perform his duty as a member of the warrior class even if it means killing his own relatives in the battle. It is better to perform one's duty, he says, even though not done well, than somebody else's duty. If Lalla has read the *Gita* intensely, as she claims in one of her verses (V 96), it is clear from her life that she sees its grounding in the patriarchal discourse. She is able to isolate metaphysical concepts that she is interested in, rejecting the prescriptive content that perpetuates caste and gender based hierarchies. For her, commitment to duty as a wife and a daughter-in-law means being confined to these roles for a lifetime without any opportunity of finding her own voice or realizing her agency. The exaltation that Arjuna has in performing his duty as a warrior

[15] The lion here refers to the desire for worldly things. Lalla brought her desires under control and then only could she proceed on her quest and achieve self-realization.

or that a brahmin priest has in spending a lifetime performing rituals and maintaining his superior status, is not validated by her personal experience. As an outsider, she has a keen awareness of the viewpoint of the privileged and its underlying assumptions; she also sees that it is based on her own exclusion from the scheme. The ideology of duty and devotion helps the male members of the warrior and priestly class maintain their class and gender privileges. When applied to women, however, it contributes toward maintaining their subordinate position in the family. The ideology of ideal wife and mother promotes the self-sacrificing ethos of women. This ethos traps a woman in relationships so that she misses opportunities to expand herself politically, spiritually, or intellectually; she is left with only "the hopelessly overcharged intensities of the personal and the domestic" (Keller 17).

Lalla emphasizes that the chain of karma can be stopped by engaging in selfless actions where the individual performs an action without being attached to the fruits of the action. She compares the path of wisdom to a kitchen garden that needs to be nurtured with self-restraint and good actions performed with detachment. As the *Gita* says: "Not by the nonperformance of actions does man reach actionlessness, nor by mere renunciations does he attain to perfection" (48). Krishna advises Arjuna to perform actions without attachment which is the only way to reach the highest truth. In some of her verses, Lalla says:

> Responsibility for one's actions one must bear
> Others share their fruit
> Without attachment, I offer my actions to the Self
> So wherever I go, it is good for me (V 80)

Lalla criticizes the practices of the brahmin elite who take great pride in their scholarly achievements which does not necessarily mean that they have a true insight into the subject they write about. Thus, she says:

You have a charming face but a heart of stone
The truth never penetrated you
Reading and writing wore out your lips and fingers
But the inner confusion never left you (V 108)

She suggests that external worship or rituals are of limited use in a spiritual journey. Objects of ritual worship, for example, kusha grass, sesame seeds, lamp or water, are unnecessary in the same way as is making offerings of animals to idols. While commenting on the goat sacrifice done in those days to appease gods and goddesses, Lalla says, it is foolish to give offerings of living creatures to dead stones; goats live on grass and water, and their wool covers our bodies to keep us warm. In yet another verse, she says, self-knowledge cannot be acquired by merely going to temples or going on pilgrimages.

A religious mendicant goes to every holy place
Seeking to attain self-knowledge
O, mind, in spite of learning do not be directionless
From a distance the grass looks greener (V 88)

Real temple, Lalla says, is within each individual and the deity one is seeking is Shiva that is one's own true nature. Reading religious scriptures, according to her, is beneficial for the beginners, but those who make a religion of recitation of scriptures are chasing illusions. She regards people who are consumed by their quest for deeper answers as fully awake and those immersed only in material reality as asleep:

Some though asleep are awake
Some while awake have fallen asleep
Some are dirty after a bath
And some even as householders are totally detached (V 130)

Lalla thus preaches that one's lifestyle or actions performed are not in themselves a guarantee for staying in ignorance or attaining enlightened perspective. Parrots can be taught to recite the name of Rama, so repetition in itself does not lead to self-knowledge. Similarly, reciting the *Gita* daily may give the aspirant the satisfaction of being engaged in a spiritual activity, but this in no way means that any progress is being made toward attaining the desired goal.

> Without discernment, O, dear, they read religious books
> As parrots recite "Rama" in a cage
> Reading the Gita becomes an excuse
> I have read the Gita and I am still reading it (V 96)

Using vivid metaphors and images, Lalla teaches people to resist following blindly the religious scriptures. She also urges them to exercise self-restraint and engage in good deeds. She brings people's attention to the need for a personal morality based on honesty and responsibility rather than on rules of conduct based on religious bigotry.

> Kill your mortal enemies—lust, anger, and desire
> Otherwise they would kill you with their arrows
> Calm them with self-restraint and good thoughts
> Recognize their nature and their power (V 127)

> Renouncing cheating, deceit, and hypocrisy
> Is the teaching I told my mind to follow
> Only One I found in everything
> Then what is wrong with eating with people from different
> castes or religions (V 56)

As a wandering ascetic, Lalla relies on the food offered to her by others who belong to a community other than her own. In the above verse, then, Lalla critiques the social practices of her time when the upper caste Hindus did not consider the food cooked by Muslims or by Hindus of lower castes as clean enough to be consumed. Lalla's emphasis on religious tolerance is in agreement with the monist Shaiva philosophy which is secular in its orientation, though it could also be a result of her interaction with Sufi mystics. For Lalla all people, irrespective of their caste, religion or gender, are equal as far as their aspiration, potential, and success in self-realization are concerned. They should, however, possess a burning desire for self-knowledge which she compares to the offering of flowers of devotion. Lalla refrains from identifying herself with any sect, or religion. Shiva consciousness, she says, is beyond these artificial divisions. People might call this state as Shiva, Keshava, Mahavir, or Buddha, but these are just different names assigned to the same reality.

> The Self may be named Shiva, Keshava, or Mahavir
> Or the lotus born Buddha
> Whatever name it may have
> May it remove worldly attachments of a weakling like me (V 20)
>
> The world is full of differences
> If you are tolerant, you will be happy
> You will end anger, hate, and animosity
> Then only will you see Shiva's face (V 105)
>
> Shiva is omnipresent
> Don't differentiate between Hindus and Muslims
> If you are clever, you will recognize your true self
> That is your real acquaintance with the Lord (V 83)

She preaches tolerance towards religious practices other than one's own. Since Shiva permeates the world, according to her, it is narrow-mindedness and fanaticism that leads to religious wars. Even though people might differ based on gender, caste, or religious creed or on the level of attainment, all are permeated with the Self or Shiva which is like a bright sun that shines equally everywhere. In a verse, she elaborates on this concept by referring to the single source of stones that serve various functions. Some stones, she says, serve as parts of the grinding stone, a tool for grinding wheat that nourishes our body, others adorn the temple altars where people go to fulfill their spiritual needs. Still others are used for building pavements for people to tread upon. Yet all types of stones come from the earth (V 99). It is the clouds of ignorance that stop the ever present illumination of one's true nature. Once the clouds disappear, the Self reveals itself in its fullness and Shiva or the ultimate consciousness is seen to pervade both the material and the nonmaterial world. She says:

> Like a fine net spread everywhere is Shiva
> Subtly permeating the physical manifestation
> If you don't see him when you are alive,
> how can you do it when you are dead?
> Through self-introspection get rid of the Self in yourself (V 102)

Lalla critiques the prescriptive religious practices of all kind. Thus, renouncing home in itself is not enough to achieve self-realization and neither is reciting prayers, chanting mantras, or turning rosary beads.

> Some renounce their home and some their hermitage
> All this is futile if the mind is not brought under control
> Meditate on your breath day and night
> And stay where you are (V 104)

> Continuous reading and reciting turned my tongue and palate sore
> Yet I did not find a practice appropriate for you
> Turning the rosary beads have worn out my thumb and finger
> Yet my mind's confusion, my dear, did not leave me (V 9)

The real practice, according to Lalla, lies in deliberate self-introspection which involves not only strengthening concentration and will, but also refusing to take for granted the received patterns of behavior as well as world view. Performing religious practices habitually might give the individual satisfaction in engaging in something spiritual but in reality would do nothing to expand the limited vision that leads to religious bigotry and non-tolerance. According to a legend, once her teacher Shri Kanth was bathing in the river, while Lalla was cleaning the outside of a pot a little upstream. Shri Kanth, puzzled, asked her how she could possibly have a clean pot if she scrubbed it only from the outside. Lalla calmly responded, how could he become pure by just bathing his body, without purifying his thoughts and feelings (Koul 1921, 306). This legend could be understood as Lalla's critique of hypocritical practices of brahmins in the name of purity, while in the secular world they were engaged in acts that were oppressive to others.

Lalla describes moderation as an important aspect in attaining the enlightened perspective. One must be moderate in drinking, eating, and clothing oneself. She does not approve of starving the body through fasting or performing religious rituals or austerities to reach spiritual goals. The real religious practice is to engage in actions that benefit others and that are performed in the spirit of detachment.

> Don't torture your body with thirst and starvation
> When the body is exhausted, take care of it
> Cursed be your fasts and religious ceremonies
> Do good to others, for that is the real religious practice (V 116)

Indulging in eating and clothing oneself will not lead to tranquillity. Leading a balanced lifestyle should ultimately be conducive to introspection and clear the path of knowledge.

Even though leading the life of an ascetic, Lalla is very much concerned about the welfare of the people and her verses are a living testimony to that fact. The message she conveys to people is to tolerate differences and to regard the self and the other as equal. However, even though Lalla participates in society from outside the periphery, it has no place for her own self-actualization. Having rejected her family, she can only exist by negating that life through reversal. Her body becomes the site of resistance that refuses to conform to the traditional gender roles. Lalla forges her own space outside the community, which ultimately turns out to be an in-between space, where she is outside patriarchal social and economic arrangements, yet tied to them through her role as teacher and social critic.

CHAPTER FOUR

Shaiva Literature and the Female Subject

KASHMIR Shaivites emphatically reject the Vedantic belief that the phenomenal world is an illusion, instead they describe it as real. As each individual's own nature lies in Shiva, liberation involves achieving awareness that both the world of inner speech and thoughts and the outer world of objects are manifestations of universal consciousness or Shiva. Thus, liberation does not mean withdrawal from the world, but it means to experience it fully, because it is an expression of Shiva consciousness. However, we see in Lalla's verses a revulsion for this world. To her liberation is only possible when one withdraws from the world and renounces all pleasures and comforts of this life. In her verses, she focuses on the transitoriness of worldly things and how important it is for the mind not to be enamored by material things. Her personal life exemplifies this philosophy.

Lalla's insistence on the withdrawal from the world in the Shaiva tradition arises from her location as a woman practitioner in a patriarchal social structure which provides no space for her to fully engage in the world by acting upon it. Various interpretations of Kashmiri Shaiva mythological and metaphysical literature have tended to suppress the potential within the Shaiva discourse for avoiding representations that subsume the female subject into the male-defined transcendent subject. In order to understand the deeper current of Lalla's thought, therefore, it is important to explore the nature of female subjectivity as it appears both in the mythological literature as well as metaphysical descriptions of the Shaiva tradition. By exposing the contradictions and discontinuities between the mythological and metaphysical representations of Shiva/Shakti duality, I hope to show that some of Lalla's verses point to a third space which goes beyond the traditional Shiva/Shakti duality. Realization of the third space, a common experience in many mystical traditions, would explain why Lalla feels so empowered in her spiritual life, even as she is an outcast in her social life. Using current feminist scholarship, especially Luce Irigaray's feminist work on western metaphysics, as a heuristic device, will allow me to explore the nature of the female subject and female desire as it appears in the Kashmiri Shaiva tradition. This analysis is essential to get a deeper insight into how Lalla's thought was shaped by the tradition while at the same time explain the contradictory position she occupies with respect to it. It also makes it possible to evaluate the relevance of her explorations into the Kashmiri Shaiva metaphysics might have for contemporary women.

The Female Imaginary and the "Logic of the Same"

Scholars have commented on the evolution of goddesses in general and the Goddess figure in particular in the Hindu tradition. The goddess worship evolved as non-brahminical divinities and religious influences were integrated into the orthodox brahminical world-view which was predominantly masculine in its imagery and symbolism. Kathleen Erndl in *Victory to the Mother* notes that vague indications of the concept of Shakti in the Vedas become more definite in the Upanishads. The epics, the *Mahabharata* and *Ramayana,* represent the transitional texts which include a number of goddesses, but merely as wives of the more powerful male gods. Erndl further points out that goddesses still have to acquire any soteriological or cosmogonic significance which begins to happen in the Puranas where goddesses are shown to participate in their male partners' activities and are sometimes depicted as dominant over them. It is in Puranic literature, then, that the concept of the Great Goddess begins to crystallize.

In a more detailed study *The Rise of the Goddess in the Hindu Tradition*, Tracy Pintchman shows that the mythology of the Vedas already contains unclearly formulated associations of goddesses with cosmogonic and cosmological functions of power and materiality. The Puranic texts, she notes, represent a conflation of the philosophical and mythological categories, which provide an ideal framework in which goddesses are made to correspond with the philosophical principles so that they begin to play an important cosmogonic role. The depiction of the Goddess as Shakti, Prakriti, and Maya makes the female goddess both the impelling as well as the material cause of creation. The Goddess from the perspective of the material creation is now the creative power or shakti which brings the universe into existence. On the other hand, from the perspective of the enlightened view, she is the delusory power or maya. The concept of maya connects the material reality (*prakriti*) with the creative power (*shakti*). In *Vaishnava* and *Shiva puranas*, Pintchman further notes, the female goddess manifests only at two levels—as Shakti she is the impelling force inherent in Brahma that creates the universe and as Prakriti she is the material cause that sustains the universe. The feminine power depicted in these texts, however, always appears as subordinate to the male deities, Vishnu or Shiva.[16]

[16] Pintchman attributes the evolution of the concept of the Great Goddess to the confluence of the philosophical and mythological cosmogonic categories that particularly involve the manifestation of the goddess as Shakti, Prakriti, and Maya. In *Shakta Purana*, for example the *Devi-Bhagavata Purana*, a third level is added to the two levels of manifestations of the Goddess that we find in Shiva Purana. The third level of manifestation transcends the function of the Goddess as the impelling as well as the material cause of creation. Now the Goddess herself is identified with the Absolute which is called Shakti, Nirguna Shakti, or primordial (*adya*) Brahman. See Pintchman, pp. 188–189.

The *Shiva Purana* describes Brahma, the god of creation, making several attempts at creation but each time it fails since it is without sexual differentiation. The idea of male and female proliferation through sexual procreation occurs to him as a result of performing austerities. Brahma's mental conception of the androgynous form of Shiva-Shakti is materialized in the body of Shiva who divides into half male and half female. He projects the female out of his body which manifests as the great goddess Shakti from whom a set of Shaktis including Sati emerge, the latter becomes the mother of womankind. Shakti, the great goddess, after performing her role in the creation of womankind withdraws into Shiva and once again becomes one with him (SP, II 1074–1078).

The implications of this myth for Hindu women can be better understood with an elaboration on the feminist theorizing in the west.

The history of western philosophy, as Jacques Derrida says, is a search for the history of the origins, the Idea, God, or the first principle which is nonderivative. Derrida deconstructs the western philosophical discourse by showing that the language is already implicated in the system under consideration. Hence it is impossible to describe something that is supposedly outside the system. Luce Irigaray focuses on yet another aspect of the same question. She looks at different discourses as conceptual systems built on phallocentric foundation which excludes the feminine. The first principle of the Western discourse, the Idea, truth, presence, or God is based on the masculine imaginary[17] which suppresses the feminine.

[17] The term "imaginary" has rich connotations in the theoretical discourses ranging from Sigmund Freud to Jacques Lacan. In Lacan, the concept becomes the basis of his theory of ego development that he describes in terms of the mirror stage characterizing the initial phase when the baby sees himself reflected in the mirror and learns to identify himself with the reflected image. The mother is the support which holds the mirror in place. In broader

In *Speculum of the Other Woman*, Irigaray focuses on the infrastructure that keeps the speculary mechanism of the western cultural imaginary in place by reading major western texts from Plato to Freud mimetically. Her psychoanalysis of philosophers exposes the buried female imaginary that stays unrepresented in these texts. In *This Sex Which is Not One*, she points out that privileging of symmetry in western culture can be best understood if language and the symbolic is regarded as a flat mirror in which the male subject sees himself reflected. She compares the female imaginary to the tain of the mirror which enables the reflection but is not itself reflected. What the female subject sees in the flat mirror is thus the inverse image which is either seen as a lack or as a masquerade, since her sex is not subject to specularization. As the masquerade, the woman sees herself in the mirror of representation in terms of the "masculine" representation of the "femininity". Thus, whereas man already is, woman must become in order to be "normal". Consequently, the woman does not see herself as the desiring subject, but as a reflection of what the man desires (1985, 129–134).

According to Irigaray, "The imaginary morphology of western rationality is characterized by: the principle of identity (also expressed in terms of quantity or ownership); the principle of non-contradiction (in which ambiguity, ambivalence, or multivalence have been reduced to a minimum); and binarism (for example, nature/reason, subject/object, matter/energy, inertia/movement)—as though everything had to be either

perspective, Irigaray shows, the unconscious, the chaotic or the undifferentiated, often conceptualized as the feminine, is the substratum out of which the conscious, the stable, the rational and the linear order of the western discourses emerges. The creation of order often takes place either by repression and non-representation of the other or by perceiving the other as a negative or an inverse image of the subject. For an extensive discussion on rationality and the imaginary in western culture, see Whitford, Chapter 3.

one thing or another" (Whitford 59). The female imaginary is thus the residue that lies outside the ordered, rational, and linear discourses of the western culture. Irigaray sees the need to create a "feminine syntax" that abandons privileging symmetry and oneness and "preclude[s] any distinction of identities, any establishment of ownership, thus any form of appropriation" (1985, 134).

The western representational systems, both discursive and symbolic, Irigaray argues, work on the "logic of the same" which means that all other elements are seen in terms of their similarity to the first principle. When the first principle is male-defined, everything outside the first principle becomes feminine or the other not only in discursive and symbolic representations, but also at the concrete level where women and nature are classified as the other.[18] Irigaray very astutely observes that the sexual difference as we see it in male-defined conceptual systems works "'within' systems that are representative, self-representative, of the (masculine) subject. Moreover, these systems have produced many other differences that appear articulated to compensate for an operative sexual indifference. For one sex and its lack, its atrophy, its negative, still does not add up to two. In other words, the feminine has never

[18]Serene Jones commenting on Irigaray's reading of western philosophers, says: "As [Irigaray] reads between the lines of the philosophers' story, she uncovers a secret, namely, that although a philosopher may claim that his or her central principle is nonderivative, the construction of its identity is a function of its interaction with the other; for without its other, the contours of its shape would be endlessly fluid. However, in order to protect the stability and a priori status of the central principle, philosophers have refused to acknowledge openly the productivity of this play of difference, for if it were admitted, the legislative authority of the center would be threatened. Irigaray refers to the sleight of hand whereby philosophers hide generative difference as the "blind spot" of Western discourse. This "blind spot" refers to that logical moment within discourse that is repressed for fear that the very pillars of discursive coherence might crumble if it came into view" (114).

been defined except as the inverse, indeed the underside, of the masculine" (1985, 159).

Her project then is to explore as to "how to secure a place for the feminine within sexual difference." However, what Irigaray does not want to do is to undertake a reversal of position and define the feminine as the first principle as many feminists have done by making the goddess figure symbolizing the feminine, as the central principle of their system (Irigaray 1985, 159). The discourse based on the feminine as the first principle also utilizes the logic of the same which means that there is only one sex in discourse and everything is appropriated to it and evaluated on the basis of its similarity to it. It is important to remember that when Irigaray speaks about the male and the female imaginary, she is not referring to the biological male and female bodies, but rather to the symbolic structure that shapes these bodies.

According to Irigaray, the suppression of the female imaginary in language and in the symbolic order that appears in myths, literature, and art has prevented women from experiencing themselves as speaking subjects. In order to promote women-as-subjects in the social arena, it is crucial that woman-as-subject is unearthed in the symbolic system and intellectual discourses. The sexual indifference, she adds, must be replaced by sexual difference which would result from the acceptance of the sexuate nature of discourses. This would allow women to become subjects and promote healthier relationship between the two sexes. Instead of one sex seeing itself reflected in the other, both men and women would experience themselves as subjects reflected in the othering of their own self rather than of the other selves.

Irigaray argues that the "the sexualization of discourse" will give voice to the suppressed other so that various discourses instead of opting for univocality and oneness will become fluid, multivocal and plural in which both the male and the female can easily alternate between the position of the subject and the object. The introduction of sexual difference in language could lead to "the possibility of a different relation to the transcendental. Neither simply subjective nor simply objective, neither univocally centered nor decentered, neither unique nor plural, but as the place—up to now always collapsed in an ek-stasis" which she calls the *copula*." Irigaray further notes that this "place may only emerge if the feminine is granted its own 'specificity' in its relation to language. Which implies a logic other than the one imposed by discursive coherence" (1995, 153-154).[19]

Irigaray's theory of the female imaginary is not an essentialist description of women in real life, but rather a reflection on how women have existed and how they have been represented in western culture for centuries. In fact, her use of elemental ima-gery, the cave, the womb, or fluids when she speaks about the buried feminine, is to avoid giving any essentialist definition of the female. The emphasis in her writings, finally, is more on the concept of inclusion of difference itself rather than on creating essentialist male and female categories; the insistence on sexual difference does not imply essentilizing the category female.

[19] Margaret Whitford attempts to untangle the relationship between Irigaray's concept of speaking subject and God who has been traditionally defined as the objective other of man. She notes, that Irigaray's "sensible transcendental" is not a conceptualization of an objective other. Rather, it points to the state of becoming or "the immanent efflorescence of the divine." One can also look at it "as the symbolic order in its *possibilities of and for transformation*, in other words, language as a field of enunciation, process, response and becoming, but a field in which there are *two* poles of enunciation so that 'I' may be male or female and so may the 'you', so that the speaker may change positions, exchange with the other sex; it follows, too, that the divine other must also be potentially of the female sex. And so we find that the sensible transcendental is also referred to as a *god*" (Whitford 47).

Irigaray's theoretical framework, if used cautiously, can help shed light on the fate of the female imaginary in the Eastern discourses, too. The caution is necessary, because the western philosophical discourse is primarily concerned with epistemology rather than ontology—with the rational subject rather than the transcendental subject.

Eastern discourses do not emphasize the rational subject, because the intellect is only one of the many attributes that constitute the self. Instead the focus shifts to consciousness that encompasses all psychological and elemental states, out of which the self emerges. Whereas Cartesian rationality presupposes a separate world out there that is perceived by the subject in terms of representations reflected in the mirror of mind, in Kashmir Shaivism the world and the mirror of consciousness are not two different realities. In Kashmir Shaivism, both the mirror of the mind and its reflection of the world get collapsed into one encompassing reality, so that there is nothing outside the mirror that gets reflected. There is no need for the other to hold the speculary mechanism in place as is the case in the western cultural imaginary. In spite of this fundamental difference, however, the specular logic that privileges the male imaginary has not escaped Kashmir Shaiva discourse.

Kashmiri Shaivite metaphysics, for example, is based on hierarchical duality in which Shiva, the transcendental Self, though supposed to be neutral, is in fact masculine in its attributes. Even though alternative narratives in the Kashmiri Shaiva literature are possible, there is a tendency to build a phallocentric discourse around the idea of Shiva/Shakti. Thus, for Kashmiri Shaivites, Shiva, which is male-defined, is the ultimate principle. Various Shaivite texts emphasize that both Shiva/Shakti are equally important because power (Shakti) can not be distinguished from the possessor of power (*Shaktiman* or Shiva). Just as the burning power is not separate from fire, the highest Shakti or *parashakti* is not separate from Shiva or

Bhairava. Since Shakti and the possessor of Shakti (*Shaktiman*) are indistinguishable, "therefore being endowed with His (i.e. *Shaktiman's*) attributes Shakti itself becomes the bearer of the same attributes" (VB 18). The *Spandakarikas* also emphasize the importance of both Shiva and Shakti principle, even as they leave us in "no doubt that it is always S[h]iva /S[h]ankara Who is said to be the supreme deity and sole reality. All that exists in either the subjective sphere of language or objective sphere of its objects of denotation is S[h]iva" (Dyczkowski SV 50).

Shiva's ultimate subject status is only possible when Shakti is subsumed into him to make space for transcendence. The absorption of Shakti into the male-defined Shiva leads to the suppression of the female imaginary in Hindu philosophical discourse which is reflected at the experiential level in ignoring women's experiences; they are denied the status of speaking subjects and excluded from spheres of activities where they can assert their subjectivity because they are seen as a threat to the self-contained male subjectivity. Ordering reality into hierarchical dualities and binaries, the Hindu discourses lead to fundamental gender splitting which reduces women to their bodies and assigns them an ultimate object status that makes them unsuitable for any direct salvation schemes of the tradition. In fact, the precondition for liberation in Indian philosophical traditions is to exclude the body. Thus, as Irigaray would say, it all starts with one sex which is indifferent to sexual differentiation. Following the binary logic, Shiva is the desired, the transcendent male defined Self which is the privileged pole and the goal in this discourse. Shiva's transcendence turns into immanence with the positing of the world as the other which is defined in feminine terms. The transcendental Self then can be realized only if the self folds back onto itself and negates the world—the feminine thus subsumed in the ultimately masculine Shiva. The description of the transcendental self in Kashmir Shaivism has not escaped the specular logic of the same where the philosopher sees his own reflection in the transcendental foundation on which he bases his system. If the foundation of the system is gendered, its constituent elements are gendered, too. The feminine Shakti that Shiva casts as the other, against which he defines and secures his boundaries is identical with him in its difference. Shaiva mythological descriptions of creation as well as philosophical discourses on the nature of reality are based on patriarchal assumptions of the logic of the same where the ultimate principle is finally unitary and masculine into which all the differences are subsumed.

Androgyny, Desire, and the Female Subject

Muriel Dimen describes patriarchy as a system of domination that differs from other systems of domination based on race or class in that "it goes directly for the jugular of social relatedness and psychological integration—desire. Patriarchy attacks desire, the unconscious longing that animates all human action, by reducing it to sex and then defining sex in the politicized terms of gender. Paradoxically however, sexuality, thus organized by gender, becomes reciprocally desire's sculptor, while gender simultaneously organizes part of desire into the self. Not only sexuality, but all manifestations of desire are thereby informed by gender; thus, the roots of desire, itself the source of personal experience, are steeped in hierarchy" (Dimen 38). The mythological literature dealing with Shiva illustrates what Dimen writes about in the western context. Shiva combines in himself two impulses, that of asceticism and eroticism. These appear as binary opposites or contradictions in the nature of Shiva who is an embodiment of both of these aspects taken to the extreme, sometimes detrimental to the balance of the universe.[20] The ascetic impulse leads to the self-contained and

[20]See Wendy O'Flaherty, *Eroticism and Asceticism in the Mythology of Siva*. The ultimate object of the Shiva myths, O'Flaherty says, is to portray balance. Thus,

self-absorbed state based on the denial of the world. This state is privileged in the duality, even though it is from the erotic impulse that his ascetic power emerges.

Shiva is lost in self-contemplation, oblivious of the external world. When touched by the arrow of desire released by god Kama, he becomes so furious that he burns Kama into ashes (SP, II, 551). The austere form of Shiva, depicted in the form of a pillar or "Sthanu, the post, withdrawn into himself, let[s] his fire burn, perpetually upward consuming and destroying all but itself" (Kramrisch 233). Shiva or *Rudra* as *Sthanu* is a figure of self-containment and asceticism, representing transcendental wholeness. The mythic representation of *Ardhanarishvara*, the union of two opposing principles, the masculine and feminine absorbed into each other, symbolizes the fulfillment of desire at one level, even as in the world of *Ardhanarishvara* there is no place for desire (Kramrisch 246). Ascetic representations of Shiva point to the existence of desire outside of him and hence always in contradictory relation with his ascetic nature which is the desired goal for liberation. Also, the sexual desire must be turned within rather than without to aid spiritual liberation.

Various Shiva myths do not in any way deal with female desire just as they ignore the need for female subjectivity. The role of Parvati (the mythological counterpart of Shakti) is to circumscribe the space of Shiva's desire and thus contain it, which is iconographically represented by *linga-yoni* symbolism. Similarly, in the secular world, the role of women has been to contain male desire, so that patriarchal structures continue uninterrupted. As the desiring power of Shiva, Shakti is the

---

on the microcosmic and macrocosmic level the "distribution and sublimation, both of which merely represent temporary phases of a more general waxing and waning. As the danger is one of energy, the ultimate solution is one of motion, not of static condition but a continuous transmutation which harnesses destructive fiery forces to drive forward the life processes" (293).

source of Shiva's integration into the world—a power over which Shiva has total control and which is identical with him in its difference. Translated into the secular realm, women are both desire and the objects of desire against which the self-contained male ego must protect itself so that its artificially constructed boundaries do not collapse. So desire must be shunned at all cost, pushed outwards till it is severed from the body. In *Shiva Purana* women are described as "a phase of illusion." Shiva's advice to ascetics is to stay away from a woman, because she is "the root of all worldly attachments. She destroys all wisdom and detachment all together" (SP II, 519).

Shiva's asceticism requires self-control, sublimation of desire, withdrawal within, and his eroticism requires fulfillment of desire through his union with Shakti, Sati or Parvati which are projections of his female half. Reading closely the Shiva cycle of myths shows that Shakti represents Shiva's agency or acting power rather than the conception of feminine power in itself. Shiva as the androgyne represents both sexes. When Sati, the mother of womankind is created, Shakti withdraws into Shiva. Shiva is the ultimate subject, who in a typically male-centered conception of subjectivity achieves self-consciousness by positing an other in the form of the female, but this female is without any body whose androgynous relationship with Shiva is based on the absence of her body. Androgyny in this context means identity based on sameness since Shakti's difference is subsumed in the sameness of Shiva. Thus the "logic of the same" operates here. Even though Shiva has divided into two, yet he is a single unity in which sexual difference has turned into "sexual indifference". In mythology even as Shiva represents the male principle and Shakti the female principle, it also labels Shiva as the subject and Shakti as the object. "While Shiva remains more or less aloof in the creation of the world, Parvati as *Shakti* is active, pervading the creation as its underlying strength and power. In this active, creative role she is sometimes identified with *prakr[i]ti* (nature), whereas Shiva is identified with *purusha* (pure spirit). As *prakr[i]ti*, Parvati represents the inherent tendency of nature to express itself in concrete forms and individual beings. In this task, however, whether as *Shakti* or *prakr[i]ti*, it is understood that Parvati either must be set in motion by Shiva or must act according to his will, wish, or design" (Kinsley 49–50).

The androgynous relationship between the two, represented in iconography in the form of a half female and half male body, is not a true depiction of androgynous state since it is based on the exclusion of femininity or the female subject altogether. Though Shakti is described as the basis of creation, she is merely Shiva's power, with which she exists in a state of non-differentiation. Shiva has subjectivity and selfhood which he maintains by separating himself from the other on the physical plane and subsuming the other in himself on the transcendental plane. In various tantric texts, Shakti or Parvati appears as Shiva's disciple who questions Shiva about the nature of reality to benefit the humankind. Thus, keeping up with the hierarchical order, Parvati occupies a position beneath Shiva and acts as an intermediary between the immanent and transcendent pole of reality.

Reservations towards the androgyny ideal which have been written for and against in western feminist discourse are understandable if we consider that they are grounded upon a basic opposition of male and female attributes. In a patriarchal culture any such opposition privileges the first masculine principle which is given primacy over its opposite that must be as similar as possible to the first. Discourses that are based on the "logic of the same" are in the end phallocentric in nature and hence, not emancipatory for women. Just as in the West, so in the East, women's voices and experiences have been suppressed and excluded from any formulation of knowledge. The philosophical as well as religious discourses are androcentric, so that women who have turned to them must once again be enmeshed in the representation of hierarchical gender relations that they find in society. Even when women are speaking subjects, as in Lalla's case, their speech is determined by patriarchal codes, to a greater or a lesser extent. Whereas in her most profound verses, Lalla attempts to go beyond binary dualism to strive for a third space, some of her verses are nonetheless coded by patriarchal discourse. For example, when she describes male and female practitioners in terms of male and female florists offering flowers of devotion, she refers to mind as the male and desire as the female florist (V 74 and 75).

The female imaginary could be said to exist in the Shakta tradition of Shaivism which is centered on the Shakti aspect of Shiva/Shakti duality. Dyczkowski notes how Kshemaraja, a Kashmiri Shaiva scholar, in his commentary on the *Spandakarikas,*[21] under the influence of *Krama*[22] philosophy, describes Shakti not only as "the source of all things," but also as "the mother of Shiva; She is such in the sense that, as the goddess of consciousness, the power of perception (*dr[i]gdevi*), She makes even S[h]iva, the highest principle, accessible to vision and hence 'generates' Him. As the creative power of consciousness, She is the *Spanda* yogi's personal object of devotion (*bhagavati*) as the creative imagination that in its genius (*pratibha*) conceives the masterpiece of creation" (SV

[21] The *Spandakarikas*, consisting of fifty three verses, summarize the teachings contained in the *Shivasutras* which are considered to have been revealed to Vasudeva. The authorship of the *Spandakarikas* is disputed. Some claim that this text was composed by Vasudeva himself, while others insist that it is the work of his student Kallata.

[22] *Krama* system is a school of Kashmir Shaivism that emphasizes Shakti, the dynamic pole of reality. Female ascetics are said to have played a crucial role in transmitting the *krama* teachings which they received through revelation. See Navjivan Rastogi 4.

54). Shakta descriptions can be interpreted as a reversal of the Shiva-centered descriptions and for that very reason contributing toward keeping the feminine still locked in the patriarchal framework of setting the other in conflictual stance to define itself. However, I will show later that, such descriptions can be reconstructed in such a way that they refrain from the binary logic and from privileging symmetry and hierarchy. The reconstruction can be regarded as a transitional move in order to write the feminine imaginary in the Eastern discourses, not as an opposite of the masculine imaginary, but as a space that refuses to be subsumed in any oppositional category. The goal finally is to describe ultimate reality in terms of a third space which is outside the binary dualism.

The third space is best illustrated in the esoteric tradition of Kashmiri Shaivism[23] where we find gender neutral depiction of ultimate reality or the Self which is described as the essential substratum of both the manifest and the unmanifest reality. However, all these gender neutral descriptions finally end up being labeled by the term Shiva. In Kashmiri Shaiva literature, the universal consciousness or Shiva consciousness is described in terms of light (*prakasha*). As Abhinavagupta explains light is formless and colorless and is capable of any shape or size. The nature of light is to illuminate and to make manifest. Light does not need anything outside of it to enable it to illuminate. The universal consciousness, too, is unconditioned and independent which through Self awareness (*vimarsha*) leads to the creation

[23] Kashmiri Shaiva literature can be divided into three categories: a. *Agamas Shastra* which includes, among others tantras like the *Malani Vijaya*, *Svachchhanda*, *Vijnana Bhairava*, *Mrigendra*, *Rudryamala*, *Netra*, and the *Shiva Sutras* with its various commentaries b. *Spanda Shastra* includes the *Spanda Karikas* with various commentaries c. *Pratyabhijna Shastra* includes Somananda's *Shiva Drishti*, Utpala's *Ishvara Pratyabhijna* , Kshemaraja's *Pratyabhijnahridayam*, and Abhinavagupta's *Tantraloka* and *Tantrasara* (Chatterji 128–169).

of the world. The *prakasha-vimarshamaya* nature of the universal consciousness allows it to be creative, dynamic, and active, allowing it to manifest itself in the diversity of the world. Liberation, then, is the recognition of one's own nature (*svasvabhava*) which is *spanda* or vibrant consciousness.

Kashmiri Shaivites describe the Self or Shiva as a painter who paints on the screen of his own consciousness or as an artist who brings forth the world for his own delight. The world is the result of the *tandava* dance of Shiva through which he expresses his pure joy and freedom. Since Shiva or the Self underlies both the self and the world, the ultimate aim for the liberated individual is to become aware of one's true nature (*svasvabhava*) through introspective contemplation and to realize the true nature of the phenomenal world. To experience the world as the aesthetic expression of Shiva is compared in the Shaiva texts to the experience of an art work. The highest art is not a realistic imitation of the external world, but the expression of joy and freedom of the Self. Abhinavagupta[24] says: "For a reader or a spectator of an artistic work, the "enjoyment of an aesthetic experience consists of a transcendental wonder (*alaukikachamatkara*) and is decidedly different from ordinary (*laukika*) knowledge such as (is produced) by memory and

[24] Abhinavagupta (10th century AD), a philosopher, literary critic, and a great Shaivite teacher wrote extensively on the role of poetry and drama to experience the bliss of the Self during moments of intense emotional experience when thought processes come to a complete halt. Abhinava wrote two influential commentaries, the *Dhvanyalokalochana* on the *Dhvanyaloka* of Anandavardhana (9th century literary critic and poet), and the *Abhinavabharati* which explicates the *Natyashastra*, a work on dramaturgy by Bharata (500 AD). In the *Abhinavabharati* while eulogizing poets, Abhinavagupta compares the poet to the creator itself, because "the poet is endowed with a power to create wondrous and unheard of things. This power arises from the grace of *Para Vak* ("Highest Speech") which is just another name for poetic imagination (*pratibha*) which has its seat in the poet's own heart, and which is eternally in creative motion (*udita*)" (quoted in AB 13).

inference."[25] The poet uses creative imagination (*pratibha*) to express the greatest freedom and joy of creation. Great poetry invokes in the reader feelings of awe and wonder. We are filled with amazement (*chamatkara*) and realize that this is how it really is. During such an experience the distance between the subject and object disappears. Time and space dissolve. The transcendence of the empirical ego leads to self-forgetfulness and total immersion in the moment.[26] As the individual engages in introspective contemplation to realize one's own nature (*svasvabhava*), she too learns to let go of the self or the ego in order to experience the reality of the Self.

To make Kashmiri Shaiva metaphysics work for women, the concept of unity in duality pervasive in various discursive and cultural representations needs to be restated as the third state that goes beyond the hierarchical binary thinking that operates on the "logic of the same". The unity in duality affirms the existence of the two poles of the duality even as they are based on the same substratum, whereas the concept of indifferential identity promotes a theory of reality in which the secondary term in the binary opposition—Shiva/Shakti, Self/self, male/female—is absorbed into the first, thus leading to the erasure of the second term, both in discursive representations and experiential domain. Scholars who admit that Kashmiri Shaiva texts contain all three descriptions—the relationship between Shiva and Shakti as unity in duality, as total identity, or Shakti as an attribute of Shiva—tend to focus on the

[25] Abhinavagupta in the *Abhinavabharati*. Quoted in AB 48.

[26] In *Towards a Psychology of Being*, Abraham Maslow uses similar terminology to describe peak experiences which are intense experience of creative, mystical, philosophical, and emotional nature. Peak experiences are the experiences of highest happiness and fulfillment. In this state perception transcends the ego and one experiences wonder, amazement, humility and even reverence. Maslow's description of peak experiences very well illustrates Kashmiri Shaiva belief that intense experience of emotions, mystical or creative in nature lead to the transcendence of the empirical ego and the experience of Shiva nature.

indifferential identity of Shiva-Shakti, thereby ignoring the alternative descriptions. The ultimate reality, according to Kashmir Shaivism, is not just consciousness, but pulsating consciousness where pulsation cannot be seen apart from what is pulsating. Shiva and its pulsation (*spanda*) belong to one moment rather than two different moments of reality and hence, exist together. Both Shiva and Shakti represent two aspects of the same reality—thus, transcendence and immanence are held together in a delicate balance as each separately represents only an incomplete description of reality. At the highest esoteric level, then, Shiva and Shakti are not bipolar opposites, but can be seen to occupy a third space that goes beyond binary dualism.

CHAPTER FIVE

Lalla's Thought
Beyond Shiva/Shakti Duality

IN order to understand the depth of Lalla's thought it is important to briefly survey the basic tenets of Kashmiri Shaiva philosophy. According to this philosophy, the ultimate reality is pure consciousness which is the fundamental ground of both the subjective as well as objective reality. Two processes closely associated with the universal consciousness are expansion or unfolding (*unmesa*) which leads to the appearance of phenomenal reality, and contraction or infolding (*nimesa)* that brings about its disappearance.

The activity of consciousness gives rise to three different states: deep sleep, dreaming, and waking. Deep sleep represents the state of unity where the universal and the individual consciousness coincide. The awareness of this unity in deep sleep is merely unconscious, but if conscious awareness of this unity exists, then it is called the "fourth state" which is achieved through introspective contemplation.

The next state of consciousness is dream state, the sphere of inner speech, containing thoughts and images which do not arise from direct interaction with the outer world as in the waking state. Hence, the dream state is different for each individual since it is unique to the person and is a part of their subjective awareness.

In the waking state, the objective sphere predominates and there is the sharp distinction between the subject and the world of objects familiar to all.

Kashmiri Shaiva philosophy conceives of universal consciousness as active. Various terms, vibration (*spanda*), Self-awareness (*vimarsha*), power (*bala*) have been used to describe its activity. Liberation, according to this tradition, lies in realizing one's own nature (*svasvabhava*) which is pure consciousness. The *Spandakarikas*, a source text for the *spanda* school, elaborate on the three types of impurities (*anavamala, mayiyamala, and karmamala*) that lead to limited vision which prevents the individual from realizing her own nature. The *anavamala* is thus the metaphysical ignorance that makes the individual experience herself as limited. The *mayiyamala* makes the limited individual forget her essential nature. The *karmamala* leads to the performance of both good and bad deeds which leave impressions that further bind the individual to the material world. On the whole, the *Spandakarikas* emphasize that the basis of the power to act (*kriyashakti*) lies in the *spandashakti* of Shiva which is one's own essential nature. Three powers associated with Shiva are will (*icchashakti*), knowledge (*jnanashakti*), and action (*kriyashakti*). The unenlightened remain unaware of their own nature, and hence, are bound by the limited vision of the empirical consciousness that confines them to the world of thoughts and ideas that are related to the objects of the world of senses. The method for gaining the enlightened perspective, according to this text, is to focus on the middle space between two thoughts in order to experience the ground of thoughts or the universal consciousness.

Whereas the *Spandakarikas* is a poetic and semi-philosophical text, Utpaladeva's *Ishvarapratyabhijna* is a systematization of *pratyabhijna* philosophy.[27] The central tenet of

[27] The first philosophic treatise on Kashmir Shaivism was *Shivadristi* composed by Somananda who lived toward the end of the eighth century. His disciple Utpaladeva wrote *Ishvarapratyabhijna,* the source text for *pratyabhijna* philosophy that was developed in Kashmir between the middle of the 9th and

pratyabhijna philosophy is once again the assertion that universal consciousness leads to the creation, persistence, and withdrawal of the universe. Liberation lies in re-cognizing (*pratyabhijna*) one's own nature. The *Shivasutras* present means of liberation which are divided into three categories. In *shambhavopaya* the experience of self-realization occurs in a sudden flash of intuition that reveals that one's own nature is the source of the outer world of diversity and the inner world of thoughts and speech. The second category is *shaktopaya,* also called *jnanayoga,* which focuses on deliberate examination of the nature of self. It involves two types of practices: contemplation of the five-fold activity of Shiva (creation, persistence, destruction, concealment, and grace) and purification of one's thought constructs. The individual consciousness is relational in nature and hence, it is dependent on the objective reality which it grasps through thought constructs woven out of language. By watching the rise and fall of thoughts in a state of passive alertness, the individual experiences her grounding in universal consciousness. The third category is *anavopaya* which involves focusing attention on the individual's body, breath, ritual, mantra, and so on. Eventually, all these practices lead to the realization that phenomenal reality emerges out of the ceaseless activity of the universal consciousness. As the individual realizes that the source of the five functions lies in one's own power (*bala*) or *spanda* which is one with universal consciousness, she experiences the fourth state of consciousness that goes beyond

---

the 11th centuries. Both Abhinavagupta (10th century) and Kshemaraja (11th century) wrote commentaries on *Ishvarapratyabhijna*. Kashmir Shaiva philosophy reached its pinnacle in the hands of Abhinavagupta who brought about a syncretism of different Shaiva schools in his voluminous *Tantraloka*, a summarization of the *Tantraloka* in *Tantrasara*, a commentary on the *Paratrishika* and several other works. His work developed Trika Shaivism into an all encompassing system which has come to be seen synonymous with Kashmir Shaivism.

waking, dreaming, and deep sleep, even as it threads through these three states.

Comparing the *pratyabhijna* and *spanda* perspectives regarding the fourth state, Dyczkowski states that "In the *Pratyabhijna* the emphasis is on a transmutation of the lower, fettered condition into its opposite by transcending all states of consciousness by recognizing the pure essence of consciousness, manifest through and as all the levels of manifestation that lead upwards to what stands beyond them, and in which they are all grounded." He notes further that in the *spanda* perspective, however,

> the Fourth state ... is that of the perceiving subject present in all states who, by 'catching hold' of himself and his basic state permeates it through all the others, even as he transcends them. Thus while the *Pratyabhijna* stresses transcendence without ignoring or minimizing immanence, *Spanda* stresses immanence grounded in transcendence....The two approaches are basically the same, just as there is no essential difference between the Fourth state and the one beyond it. The former is the latter in relation to the other states. It is the condition of consciousness which, pervading the other states, unites them together, as does a thread the flowers of a garland. As such it is the condition of the perceiver which depends equally on the perceiver's detachment from the other states and his simultaneous presence in all of them (SV 193–194).

This distinction is important to remember as we explore Lalla's thought since she shows a leaning toward the *pratyabhijna* perspective and seems to emphasize transcendence, but unlike it, ignores the significance of immanence. This attitude is also reflected in her austere lifestyle and her approach to her bodily needs. The body is only important as long as it serves as a means of transcendence.

Lalla's verses can be divided into three groups—the first group deals with the need for finding means to overcome her limited vision that binds her to the material reality. The second group of verses represents her experience with sustained introspective contemplation. Some of these verses describe the advanced stages of her practice when she realizes that threading through her ego-consciousness is the universal consciousness that can only be recognized (*pratyabhijna*) in a state of introverted contemplation when the activities of the body, mind and senses are brought to rest. In the third group of verses she turns her attention outwards as she realizes that her own essential nature (*svasvabhava*) is also the basis of the world outside. She feels compelled to take the role of a teacher in order to instruct others on the nature of limited knowledge and means to overcome it to achieve higher levels of awareness.

We cannot forget that her verses were addressed to common people in the countryside who most probably would have had a hard time understanding the highly esoteric vocabulary of Kashmiri Shaivism. For this reason, Lalla used metaphors and similes from day to day life that were directly accessible to the common people. Her verses also reflect her awareness of the mixed audience that she was addressing. Accordingly, some of her verses speak about the need for devotion to Shiva and then there are others that describe Shiva as the transcendental reality permeating the physical reality, and yet others focus on the need to do away entirely with duality of all kinds in order to find a totally new space for the actualizing self. The ultimate goal in these handful of verses, then, is to go beyond the meditation and the object of meditation to achieve a state beyond thought constructs.

Lalla's approach can be classified under the third category *anavopaya* in that she begins with the limited individual (*anu*) who is deeply attached to the objects of the senses. Intially, she strongly identifies with her psycho-physiological complex which is held together by the intellect, the ego, and the mind. The *Shivasutras* point out that the individual consciousness is imprisoned in the world that is created out of thought constructs. The self gets attached to these constructs and identifies with the reality which is created out of words. Becoming attached, it is affected by states of pleasure and pain which create impressions that further bind the self to a world that appears divided and separate. Lalla refers to the five principles (*pancha-mahabhutas*) of experience of the physical world, solidity, aeriality, vacuity, liquidity, and formativity, the ten organs that include the five organs of sense perception (*jnanendriyas*) and the five of action (*karmendriyas*), as well as mind (*manas*) arising from ego consciousness (*ahamkara*). If all were brought under control, self-knowledge would be achievable:

What will I do with the five, ten, and eleven
They have all emptied out the cauldron
If all had come together and pulled the rope
Then the eleven would not have lost the cow (V 6)

When I was attached to the ego consciousness
You remained hidden from me
Time passed in my search for you
When I saw you within
You and I were united in ecstasy (V 69)

The first step toward self-knowledge involves getting rid of the ego consciousness or I-ness and opening up to Shiva consciousness. Also, focusing on the transitoriness of material things can be used as an aid to turning one's attention away from sense objects. Whereas in the *bhakti* tradition external deity and objects of worship are used to gain spiritual experience, in the Shaiva tradition external objects of worship are replaced by sustained contemplation on the Self. Since the attention constantly slips out of the five senses, extreme will power must be cultivated to proceed with the practice. Lalla often compares the restless mind to a horse that is galloping away:

The mind-horse wanders all over
With the flicker of an eyelid it travels a hundred thousand leagues
She who holds the reins with self-restraint and discrimination
Succeeds in controlling the inhaled and exhaled breath (V 89)

Her verses frequently comment upon the dynamism between Shiva and Shakti in terms of the interplay between the self (the finite consciousness) and Shiva or the Self (the universal consciousness). The realization of the Self within oneself, *atmavyapti,* and the realization of the Self as the substratum of the outside world, *shivavyapti,* is the constant message that she tries to impart through her poetry. To her, liberation means to develop an enlightened perspective wherein the world is experienced as the expression of Shiva. The two realities, Lalla says, seem to exist apart only from an unenlightened perspective, while the enlightened perspective reveals that both the empirical and universal, as well as the manifest and the unmanifest are interwoven. The manifest world thus arises out of the womb of the unmanifest like a wave rises from the ocean, only to recede back into it. The reality of the wave cannot be seen apart from the reality of the ocean.

Lalla describes Shiva or the Self as the substratum of the phenomenal reality. She compares it to the salt that is dissolved in water. Just as it is not possible to see the salt dissolved in water, so it is impossible, from a limited perspective, to experience the Self as the basis of reality. Evaporation of water leaves behind salt; similarly, contemplation of the Self when worldly desires and preoccupations are left behind leads to self-realization. In order to clarify the relationship of the Self to the self, Lalla uses the metaphor of water and its two other forms as they appear in nature: ice and snow. When the clouds dispel, and the sun reveals its face both ice and snow melt and turn into water, even though as ice and snow they have their own unique properties as well as modes of existence specific to their conditions.

> Cold changes water into ice or snow
> Discernment shows the three states
> Though different are not really different
> When the sun of consciousness shines

The plurality is dissolved into oneness
Then the universe appears throughout permeated with Shiva (V 39)

Shiva's obscuring power is seen here as clouds that limit one's vision. When the sun of consciousness shines, or in other words when the individual consciousness realizes its oneness with the Self, the subject/object duality is erased and the Self which is the quintessential nature of both is revealed in its fullness.

In yet another verse, Lalla uses the example of a grinding stone to clarify the relationship between the self and the Self. She compares the Self to the axle of the grindstone which provides the force to move the flat stones that grind the grain. For the wheat to move into the middle portion to be ground between the flat stones, the axle must be in motion. Without this motion, the motion of the grinding stone and consequently, that of the wheat would come to a standstill. Whereas in the previous verse, the plurality of distinct states dissolves into sameness, in this verse the uniqueness of each constituent part remains intact. The movement of the axle becomes the formative principle that brings about the motion of the flat stones which pulls in the wheat to be ground into fine flour. The grindstone thus becomes a metaphor for human fulfillment where to live an enlightened existence, the self-aware individual must also take control of the axle of the grindstone, the higher Self, in order to experience fully the dynamic weaving of the world from the light of consciousness itself.

In most verses, Lalla repeatedly stresses the continuity between the self and Shiva and between Shiva and the world. Individuals are not isolated islands in the ocean of consciousness, but rather waves in the ocean, so their existence is intricately bound up with the reality out of which they emerge. She captures this continuity in an image of Shiva in the form of a net spread over the entire phenomenal world, in the meshes of which the individual existence takes shape. Her verses urge people to cultivate a double vision to realize how the lived world is a construction built out of stories which shape both the social as well as the spiritual reality. Through cultivating double vision, the individual is involved fully in day to day activities while at the same time always aware of the constructed nature of material reality. The current that runs through Lalla's verses reflects her belief that enlightened perspective can be realized through one's own striving, even as notions of grace and ignorance are an important part of her thought. When the individual is continually aware that she is the agent of all five operations, she develops the insight to enjoy the world of diversity as the play of consciousness.

Controlling the mind and the senses is followed by mastering breathing. Some of Lalla's verses deal with actual practices in the Kashmiri Shaiva tradition which focus on controlling the *pranashakti* or vital breath.

> After wandering in ten directions, I found the true path
> Through breath control I penetrated the void
> Shiva I saw permeating everywhere
> When I shut the six (five sense organs and mind) and the three (openings)
> I found Shiva as the root cause of all (V 54)

This method of meditation involves focusing within, watching the inhalation (*apana*) and exhalation (*prana*) which is combined with the cessation of all thoughts. The *Vijnanabhairava* gives innumerable techniques for this purpose. And one of them is *hamsah* which involves meditation on the middle space between the in-breath and out-breath (VB 22). Fixing one's attention on the space between two thoughts is yet another extension of this practice. Instead of moving from thought to thought, the practitioner focuses on the space between two thoughts to experience the ground out of which all thoughts arise. Through constant absorption in *hamsa*, Lalla experiences that the Self or Shiva is the essential nature of both the outer world of diversity and the inner world of contemplating self.

Regarding this practice, Lalla says:

The region of the navel is naturally ablaze
The breath moves up to the throat
To the *brahmarandhra* where the river flows
For this reason, *Huh* (inhaled breath) is cold
And *Hah* (exhaled breath) is hot (V 32)

I took the reins of the mind-horse
Through practice I learned breath control
Then only the orb of moon melted and flowed down into my body
Nothingness merged with nothingness (V 34)

In some verses she refers to yet another practice that deals with one's absorption in the sound of Om.[28] Lillian Silburn shows that Lalla's references to Om in her verses can actually be traced to a practice given in the *Svachchhandatantra* which concerns the ascent of the vital breath through the psychic centers of the body while the syllable Om is sounded. The three syllables of the sounding of Om are A, U, and M which are associated with psychic centers located in heart, throat and the

[28] In tracing the history of the sacred *mantra* Om in India, Mark Dyczkowski points out that in Vedic times Om was recited in the beginning of the Vedic hymns and regarded as the male seed that fertilized the female hymn. In Upanishidic times, the three syllables of the sound Om, AUM, came to symbolize three states of consciousness—waking, dreaming, and deep sleep. In the tantric literature, this symbolism was extended even further in that the resonance at the end of the sounded AUM itself was seen to incorporate subtler levels of awareness which were divided into different phases: the point (*bindu*), the half moon (*ardhachandra*), the limit (*nirodhika*), the sound (*nada*), the unstruck sound (*nadanta*), the energy (*shakti*), pervasiveness (*vyapini*), the equal one (*samana*) and the transmental (*unmana*) (SV 252).

vault of the palate respectively.[29] The three syllables are also associated with three states of consciousness—waking, dreaming, and deep sleep and the three deities, Brahma, Vishnu, and Rudra (a form of Shiva). Lalla's verses do not give actual techniques, but rather use metaphorical language to convey her own experiences of altered states of awareness. These reveal to her that mystical insights into ultimate reality refuse to be contained in the reality assigned to the deities Brahma, Vishnu, and Rudra—the creator, the preserver and destroyer of the universe, according to the Hindu mythological literature.

> Shiva is the horse and Vishnu is the saddle
> And Brahma is on the stirrups
> A yogi through yogic practice recognizes the One
> Who is riding on this horse (V 45)
>
> The unstruck sound of Om
> All permeating, whose abode is void
> With no name, no color, no caste, no form
> Self-introspection reveals it as the unsounded resonance
> That is the deity who can ride the horse (V 46)

In elaborating on the significance of the sounding of Om in Kashmiri Shaiva literature, Dyczkowski explains that the resonance at the end of Om is described as passing through the phases of the point (*bindu*) and half moon (*ardhachandra*). The point represents the state when Shiva and Shakti are united. It is a concentrated point of energy which belongs to the phase of immanence and holds the entire objective sphere in potential form within. The realization of the point *(bindu)* occurs in a state of introversion, hence, it belongs to the subjective sphere. However, objectivity still predominates here. As objective awareness withdraws further, the point (*bindu*) changes into

[29]In her study *Kundalini*, Lilian Silburn shows that awakening *kundalini* and experiencing its ascent up the spine to the *sahasrara* constitutes the fundamental practice of Kashmir Shaivism.

the half moon (*ardhachandra*) which becomes a gateway to yet subtler levels of awareness that must cross the threshold called the limit (*nirodhika*). Beyond the limit, there are yet more phases: the sound (*nada*), the unstruck sound (*nadanta*), energy (*shakti*), pervasiveness (*vyapini*), equal one (*samana*), and transmental (*unmana*). Going beyond the six phases into and beyond the seventh transmental phase is the space of highest awareness which is that of undivided light. This state is that of the supreme *shiva paramashiva* which has been described in the *Svachchhandatantra* as the state of being (*bhava*) which is Non-Being (*abhava*). It has also been given the name of nothingness or void (SV 252–255).

Lalla's mastery of the above practice is indicated by the legend about her which describes her teacher's amazement at the intensity of her austerity during the forty day fast of *chandravana*. On the full moon day, she enters a clean room, stands in an earthen pot and covers her head with another such pot. As the moon wanes, her body diminishes in size, until on the fifteenth day the two pots, the top and the bottom, join each other. Sri Kanth, out of curiosity, lifts the lid and sees trembling quicksilver inside. As the moon waxes, Lalla's body begins to increase in size until on the full-moon day she regains her old size (Koul 1921, 312).

The above legend, perhaps related as a story by Lalla herself, symbolically represents the essence of Kashmiri Shaiva teachings. The rising and falling of cosmic cycles as well as individual moments of cognition and perception represent the expansion (*unmesa*) and contraction (*nimesa*) of consciousness. The recurrent cosmic cycles, the rising and setting of the sun, are self-perpetuating processes that are integrally related to the individual perception of these processes. The five-fold functions of Shiva are repeated in a limited way at the individual level as the individual engages in activities of cognition and perception. On the individual level, however, the powers of universal consciousness become a means of bondage. As Kashmiri Shaiva texts point out, it is the obscuration power of Shiva that leads to the diversity in the world. Those who get entangled in this diversity without discovering its grounding in universal consciousness remain impervious to the continuity between the subjective reality of inner thoughts and contents of the objective reality.

Abhinava writes in the *Tantraloka*: "S[h]iva, the agent of the five operations of creation, persistence, destruction, grace and obscuration is the conscious nature. Worship, the recitation of Mantra, initiation and Yoga are eternally manifest for the yogi who has realized that he himself is, in the fullness of his freedom, the agent of the five operations." Thus, the most important teaching is that "we ourselves are, by virtue of our own inherent freedom, the agents of the (five operations) of creation".[30] Whereas the first three functions of Shiva, creativity, persistence, and withdrawal, occur at both cosmic and individual level, the last two, grace and obscuration, are intimately tied to the individual striving to realize one's own nature (*svasvabhava*). On the individual level, the moment of creation arises out of mental perceptions as one's attention is focused on inner objects of thought or external objects of perception. The enjoyment of the object of attention is the moment of persistence. And when the objective sphere is assimilated or absorbed in pure consciousness and lies there as if in a potential form, the state is called reabsorption or withdrawal. The objects of mental perception and cognition leave behind impressions that arise if they are not withdrawn completely in consciousness. This results in concealment or obscuration so that the objective reality is experienced as separate and disconnected from oneself. The moment of grace (*anugraha*) is realized, when one develops the awareness and experiences one's own nature as the

[30] Abhinavagupta in the *Tantraloka*. Quoted in SV 179.

ground of both the subjective and objective sphere.

In the legend about Lalla and the pot, the transformation of Lalla's body into a ball of vibrating quicksilver symbolically represents her introspective state as she experiences expansion of her consciousness. Lalla's body does not dissolve into the blankness of nothingness, but is turned into vibrant quicksilver, a metaphor for the higher state of consciousness, also called the Fourth state. The image presents the immanence and transcendence in tension, leading to the experience of the third space which goes beyond the binary dualism. In this state, the distinction between the subject and the object disappears and the empirical consciousness transcends the objective reality.

Transgressing the distinctions between the inside and outside, the subject and object leads to the opening up of an entirely new space which refuses to be contained in any dualistic conceptual framework. Elaborating further on this new space, Lalla says:

> Speech or mind, manifest or transcendental have no existence there
> Yogic silence has no place there
> Shiva and Shakti don't live there
> Seek whatever is left beyond it, this is your lesson (V 86)

The most profound of Lalla's verses, then, try to represent an experience which is unrepresentable since it goes beyond all thought constructs, dualities, names and attributes. Even as Lalla's verses make references to Shiva as a male deity, the underlying current of her experiences is best represented by those verses that portray Shiva as the transcendental reality which is beyond any anthropomorphic representations, a reality that goes beyond subject-object duality since it is the essential ground of both. The difficult task that Lalla faces is how to represent this reality using language that always objectifies what it represents. Also, any attempt to describe the metaphysical reality that exists outside the linguistic and epistemological structures of a culture is already influenced by the thought structures and language of the culture that attempts to describe it. Finally, she describes this state by simply saying what it is not. Lalla speaks about this final state in terms of nothingness coming in touch with nothingness.

> Neither I or you nor the meditation or the object of meditation exists
> The all-doer forgets itself
> The blind find this meaningless
> The wise become one with this supreme state (V 35)

In a related verse, Lalla says,

> The sun sets, the moon shines
> The moon vanishes, consciousness remains
> Consciousness disappears, then nothingness remains
> And the physical, spiritual, and metaphysical merge into nothingness (V 44)

The sun illuminates the world of objects—the setting of the sun then represents introspective state when the individual withdraws attention from the objective sphere and rests in the subjective sphere which in this verse is compared to the shining of the moon.

In the *Spandakarikas*, similar verses appear:

> Once entered that state which (the yogi) takes as his support and firmly resolves that: "I will surely do whatever He [Shiva] says,' both the sun and moon set, flowing the ascending way, into the channel of *sus[h]umna*, once abandoned the sphere of the universe.
>
> Then in the great sky, when the sun and the moon dissolve away, the dull minded (yogi is cast down) into a state of deep sleep. The awakened however remains lucid [V 23, 24, 25]. (SV xvi)

Lalla's reference to the setting of the sun and the moon also refers to the practice which involves the control of vital breath and its ascent through the psychic centers. The setting of the sun and moon could represent two currents *prana* (*surya* or sun) and *apana (chandra* or moon) that join in the middle channel (*sushumna*) as the vital breath ascends upwards and develops into the concentrated point and on to the half moon, then breaking through the limit (*nirodhika*), and on to yet subtler levels of awareness where the universal subjectivity predominates. As the individual reaches higher states of awareness, Lalla says, it is possible to let go of this subjective sphere and experience a state when all dualities are transcended so that the physical, spiritual, and the metaphysical all come together in the experience of the new state.

Lalla also occasionally describes the process of realizing the highest state in terms of crossing six forests or six paths and seizing the seventh. The references once again are to the practices mentioned before and the ultimate goal is always to realize the state of nothingness or non-being.

> After traversing six forests, I awakened the orb of the moon.
> By controlling my breath, I gave up attachment toworldly things
> I burned my heart in the fire of love
> Thus I found Shankar (V 42)
>
> I became absorbed in the sacred syllable Om
> I burned myself like coal
> After traversing six paths, I seized the seventh
> Then only I, Lalla, reached the abode of light (V 43)

The *Svachchhandatantra* discusses the development of the syllable Om in terms of crossing seven voids, the first six of which are unstable. These voids must be transcended in order to arrive at the seventh which is free of all states; it is the highest void which represents "non-being" as opposed to "being". The notion of non-being or emptiness, Dyczkowski points out, has not been unique to the Buddhist literature; it is very much present in Shaiva texts where it has been used to describe the Indeterminate consciousness which is beyond different states of consciousness while at the same time implicit in them. The Indeterminate consciousness though mostly described in positive terms, is also a few times described as Non-Being and is "equated with S[h]iva, understood as both transcendent Non-being and yet present at the same time in all things as their essential nature in the form of 'pure Being'" (SV 211). Thus, "Non-being is beyond contemplation, and its domain is beyond the universe, free of the mind, intellect and the rest, it is devoid of reason and doctrine. It is the imperishable Lord, beyond perception and the other means of knowledge, beyond all reason and authority, free of bondage and Mantra, omniscient, omnipresent, tranquil, pure, and free of limitations."[31]

Elaborating on the concept of "non-being" or "nothingness" in Kashmir Shaivism, Kshemaraja describes it as the nothingness of fullness instead of that of emptiness of Madhyamika Buddhism. He refers to the following verses of the *Spandakarikas* which state: "Nothingness can never be an object of contemplation because consciousness is absent there. (It is a mistake to believe that one has perceived nothingness) because when reflection (subsequently) intervenes one is certain that 'it was.' Therefore consider that to be an artificial state similar to deep sleep. That Principle is forever perceived and is not remembered in this way." Thus, if ultimate reality is total void where the subject, knowledge, and the object of knowledge all merge into nothingness, then how can one recollect the experience of such a state. Kshemaraja finally concludes, that the *Spandakarikas* express only one view and that is "one should abide in every state in the firm conviction that one's own authentic nature (*svasvabhava)* is S[h]ankara Himself. Nor should one be lax at all in this, but rather constantly strive to dispel one's own ignorance, for in no state of being is S[h]iva's nature unmanifest" (SV 71).

Lalla refers to the experience of 'Non-being' (*abhava*) as nothingness (*shunya*) in her verses not in negative or nihilistic terms, but more to represent a space that cannot be contained

[31] From the *Svachchhandabhairavatantra*. Quoted in SV 211.

in any dualistic categories. The experience of nothingness is a mystic experience. The metaphor of touch can be used to understand the experience in which the relationship between the Self and the self is not of indifferential identity but rather an unfolding of the unity, where each state has its own reality. When texts describe mystic experience as merging of the individual consciousness with the ultimate consciousness, they are still following unity as the identity model of reality. The metaphor of touch would be a more appropriate term to describe this experience since it better represents the dynamic nature of reality and the active encounter involved when two different dimensions of experience come in contact.[32] While

[32]While elaborating on women's relationship to mysticism in the West, Luce Irigaray notes that the mystic discourse has provided the only space for women where they can express themselves so publicly. They break out of the self contained enclosure where hierarchies and dualities rule, and find themselves in a space where the "distinction between inside/outside [is] transgressed" and where the logic of "the self-identity-as-same" does not operate (Irigaray 1985 191-192). In fact, the mystic's "'God' goes beyond all representation, however schematic in its approximation" (1985, 197). Irigaray compares the experience to an "abyss that swallows up all persons, all names, even proper names. For in fact all properties and (proprieties) will have to be shed to continue this penetration...And which is mixed in a jouissance so extreme, a love so incomprehensible, an illumination so unbounded that un-knowledge thereby becomes desire" (1985, 194–195). The experience of the unknowable which is incapable of being articulated in discourse has a sense of immediacy. "In a deeper unity than the still, already, speculative unity that underlies the sense of these wrenching contradictions. The bottom, the center, the most hidden, inner place, the heart of the crypt to which 'God' alone descends when he has renounced modes and attributes" (Irigaray 1985, 196). Irigaray describes the mystic experience as an essentially feminine experience, and she uses the metaphor of touch as the most appropriate to represent it, since in this experience both the individual "soul" and the unknown or the "nothingness" touch one another without one being lost in the other. Thus, she says, it is the "path of touch that still guides us in our ecstatic transports". In a lyrical elaboration, Irigaray writes: "A living mirror, thus, am I (to) your resemblance as you are mine. We are both singular and plural, one and ones,

referring to the expansion of consciousness, the *Spandakarikas* state: "From that (expansion) arises the point (*bindu*), from that sound (*nada*), from that form (*rupa*), and from that taste (*rasa*) which disturb the embodied soul" (SV xvii). This stanza does not refer to the sensation of touch as an impediment to achieving higher states of awareness. According to Abhinavagupta, this exclusion points to the fact that higher levels of awareness could in fact involve the sensation of touch. Thus, he says: "Smell, taste, and color reside in a subtle state in the Earth element, in the principles up to the constitutive qualities (*guna*) and up to the end of Maya, respectively. Thus, a certain subtle tactile sensation, which yogis constantly aspire to achieve, (is experienced) at the end (and within) the principle of Power. At the end of this sensation the power of awareness (*samvitti*), which is the pure Sky of Consciousness, (becomes manifest). He who is established in this attains the supreme self-illuminating (state of consciousness)."[33] Even as Lalla in some of her verses describes her experiences in terms of two dimensions of reality coming in touch with each other, in most of her verses, she describes this experience only in terms of her realization of transcendence.

> Through constant practice the objective reality is withdrawn
> The world of forms and colors suddenly merges with void
> When the void disappears nameless consciousness remains
> This is my teaching, O Pandit! (V 85)

As the above verse indicates, she does not seem to see her embodiment as an essential prerequisite for the experience of transcendence and perhaps for that reason Shiva and Shakti

---

provided that nothing tarnishes the mirrors that fuse in the purity of their exchange. Provided that one, furthermore, does not exceed the other in size and quality. For then the other would be absorbed in the One (as) to infinity" (1985, 196–197).

[33] From Abhinavagupta's *Tantraloka*. Quoted in SV 252.

continue to occupy two extreme ends of the polarity in her material existence, even as she transcends the polarity at another level. Lalla's choice of images and metaphors, therefore, more often than not point toward creating a disenchantment with worldly things, even as a few illustrate the joy of liberated perspective.

> The consciousness is new and the moon is new
> I saw the whole universe moment by moment renewed
> Ever since I, Lalla, cleansed my body and mind
> I, Lalla, have become ever renewed (V 60)

> In the midst of being lost, I lost the sense of being lost
> After being lost I found myself in this worldly ocean
> Laughing and playing, I attained all-pervading Self
> This philosophy became a part of me (V 29)

The above two verses reflect a sense of lightness and joy with which she views the world which is still trapped in social arrangements that leave her no space to creatively express her freedom. For Lalla, her verses are the only means for expressing her joy as she advances in her practice.

The most sublime art, as Abhinava says, is not a realistic representation of the phenomenal world, but the expression of pure joy and freedom of the Self which leads to the *rasa* of peace.[34] The *shanta rasa* is the highest form of aesthetic delight because it can lead to the experience of the ultimate aim in human existence which is liberation (DL 525). The basic mental state that corresponds to *shanta rasa* is detachment

[34] The *rasa* theory of ancient India deals specifically with the nature of aesthetic pleasure. The literal meaning of *rasa* is taste, flavor, fluid, or sap, but it also means aesthetic pleasure or delight. Bharata's *Natyashastra* identifies only eight *rasas*—erotic (*shringara*), comic (*hasya*), pathetic (*karuna*), furious (*raudra*) heroic (*vira*), terrible (*bhayanaka*), odious (*bibhatsa*), and marvelous (*adbhuta*). These eight *rasas* correspond to eight basic mental or emotional states, for example, delight (*rati*), laughter (*hasa*), sorrow (*shoka*), anger (*krodha*), heroism (*utsaha*), fear (*bhaya*), disgust (*jugupsa*), and wonder (*vismaya*).

(*vairagya*), so the aesthetic delight that it produces arises from "the complete cessation of desires, that is, yearnings for objects of sense, and may be called an indifference to worldly things (*nirveda*)" (DL 521). Lalla's more profound verses exemplify the *rasa* of peace which she suggestively conveys in her cryptic metaphors. Lalla uses similes and metaphors in beautifully crafted utterances to express the insights she has into the nature of reality. In a move in which the inner becomes the outer and the outer inner, her verses are a result of outpouring of inner experiences which, having crystallized into words, in turn have the power to bring about an inner change in others. Lalla says:

I did not pause for the right moment
I did not trust anything
The wine I, Lalla, drank was my own verse
I caught the inner darkness, gathered it
Tearing it into shreds (V 148)

The aesthetic delight that Abhinava writes about in his work on poetry and drama is not available to Lalla as she has turned away from the world. Even though Lalla embodies the state of detachment with the world and hence, possesses the ability to experience it in its fullness, yet there is a deliberate attempt on her part to stay locked out of any aesthetic experience of the world. Her most profound verses then reflect her desire to lose herself in mystical experience rather than to use it as the ground to lead a more fulfilling material existence. In one of her verses, she says:

Impurities from my mind were wiped away like that from a mirror
Then only did I attain self knowledge
I saw Shiva near me
He is everything, and I am nothing (V 68)

As a hermit I came to this world
Through mediation on the Self I attained realization
No one will die to me, and I will die to nobody
Death and life are the same (V 37)

Her utterances are thus richly phrased verses to teach people to lead a better life. The insights that she gains in the spiritual realm do not in anyway enrich her life in the material realm in terms of allowing her to live a fulfilling and creative life. The two realities remain separate because of the contradictory position she occupies.

Lalla's poetry occupies an important place in women's literary history, not only in India, but also in the world, since it expresses a woman's resistance to patriarchal norms in the only way that was available to her in the historical period that she occupied. In spite of personal unhappiness, Lalla appears as a woman who had faith in her vision and who pursued her path even in the face of obstacles that she encountered. The life of a wandering ascetic is not the easiest one, yet she continuously pursued metaphysical questions that have intrigued both men and women from immemorial times. The path she was forced to take though was very much determined by the discursive as well as social formations of the patriarchal Kashmiri society. Even within the constraints, however, she felt the need to contribute in the only way she could by serving as a beacon of light to oppressed people. She urged them to have courage to seek their inner vision, instead of leading a life that is governed merely by social expectations. Through her verses, Lalla has inspired both women and men for centuries to model their lives on a vision of reality that has potential for creating a better society and thereby promoting equality, mutual respect, and caring. We can look at Lalla's verses then as an instrument of change—an inner change—that must go hand in hand with any external political change of society. For that reason, then, Lalla's verses are as relevant today, as they were more than six centuries ago.

CHAPTER SIX

The Ocean and the Waves
The Dancer and the Dance

KASHMIRI Shaiva philosophy, a life-affirming metaphysics, presents a contradiction for women, because their lives have not found affirmation in traditional Indian society which ties them to sex roles instead of giving them opportunities for self-actualization. Women like Lalla who have felt a deep need to explore metaphysical questions, have done so only at the expense of renouncing the world which is oppressive to their self-actualization. Lalla's verses repeatedly point out the futility of observing religious practices which include asceticism and renunciation. In one of her verses, she says that even householders can achieve self-realization if they work hard at it. Her own life, however, contradicts the message in her teachings.

Lalla justifies her renunciation of the world by describing it as an illusion which is surprising considering the fact that she is a Shaiva practitioner. Kashmiri Shaivites explicitly reject the position taken by nondualist Vedantins that the world is an illusion or Maya. Nondualist Vedantins believe that there is only one reality which is transcendental and inactive Brahmin. Once ignorance is removed, the world appears as what it actually is—Brahmin. For example, in darkness it is easy to mistake a rope for a snake, but once light shines on the rope, the illusion is dispelled. Kashmiri Shaivites, on the other hand, view all manifest reality as real because it represents the unfolding of consciousness. The unfolding gives rise to diversity and infolding to withdrawal into the unity that holds universe in a potential form. No two different moments or two different orders of reality exist, but only one moment with two aspects where one has the other implicit in it. As Abhinava says: "The Self is the abiding state (*sthiti*) of the light of consciousness, it is partless consciousness which, being such, has laid hold of every power. Concealing its own glory, its nature becomes that of the fettered soul, while, by making the essential nature of the light of the Self clearly evident, it is liberated."[35] Through the cultivation of the self as the Self one realizes that the universal consciousness constitutes the ground of the three states of consciousness, deep sleep, dreaming, and waking, even as it abides in the fourth which transcends the three states.

The efficacy of the notion of unity in duality or on a broader scale unity in multiplicity is closely related to what perspective is used to describe the two aspects of reality that are interwoven. The traditional interpretation of Shaivism has been to regard liberation as the realization of some eternal state which is changeless, timeless absolute—the state of Shiva consciousness. The aim of liberation then is to attain to this state in order to escape from the ravages of time which brings decay and death. For example, the commentators of the *spanda* doctrine admit that the ultimate consciousness and its vibration belong to one moment rather than two different moments of reality, but they also insist that it is ultimately Shiva who is the eternal agent of the cosmic process as well as individual experience. Dyczkowski, however, points out that the original doctrine of *spanda* did not make finer distinctions in its description of the ultimate reality. In the *Spandakarikas*, in fact, there is no contradiction seen in describing Shiva as both transcendent and immanent in all states of consciousness and yet, whose highest state of awareness transcends all states. According to the *Spandakarikas,* he continues, Shiva

[35] Quoted in SV 220.

> is transcendentally immanent, with the stress being on His immanence as the experiencing subject (*bhoktr*) who, divested of all egoity, is not the individual soul (*purus(h)a*) nor the individual perceiver (*grahaka*) but his own personal fundamental state (*svasthiti*) or being (*svasvabhava*). Engaged in the act of perception, he is also the pure agency (*kartrta*) which, although omniscient and omnipotent, is not centered on individual objects of perception or products of action, but is the universal underlying ground (*adhisthatr*) and activity (*samanyaspanda*). ....Self realization is the astonishing insight into one's own fundamental state of being as S[h]iva in both domains of subjectivity and objectivity...the liberated condition is the achievement of a state of pure enjoying subjectivity (*bhoktrta*)....The liberated yogi thus conforms to S[h]iva's state which, beyond the opposites of subject and object, pleasure and pain, is the subject who enjoys the cosmic sport of the cycle of His universal manifestation. (SV 185–86)

The original *spanda* doctrine thus represents the middle ground between the Shiva-oriented *pratyabhijna* philosophy and the Shakti-oriented *krama* system of Kashmiri Shaivism. Even though *spanda* theory could easily be interpreted as describing ultimate reality as the tension between transcendence and immanence, the commentators of the *Spandakarikas* have tended to emphasize the transcendental aspects of this system. Thus, Shiva continues to be the master and the source of the empirical reality.

The most empowering interpretation of Shaivism would be to define liberation in processual terms where self-realization is neither to be lost in the transcendent and restful Shiva nor to find oneself limited to the domain of Shakti. In the *krama* school of Kashmir Shaivism, the ultimate reality is depicted in terms of an eternal self-perpetuating succession of moments (*krama*) in the consciousness. Whereas the *pratyabhijna*, and ultimately the *spanda* system, are Shiva oriented and focus on the transcendental pole of reality where liberation means recognition of the original unity, the *krama* system with its Shakti-orientation supports the processual nature of reality, emphasizing diversity within the monist framework. The *krama* system distinguishes between the sequences of emergence (*srishtikrama*), persistence (*stithtikrama*), destruction (*samharakrama*), and a fourth state called the inexplicable (*anakhyakrama*) that includes them all in the unity of consciousness as process. As Navjivan Rastogi points out, "*krama* is more closely connected with immanent reality and interprets immanence as an essential expression of transcendence" (5). Liberation, according to the *krama* system, means to be aware that permeating the diverse phenomena is the unity whose nature is succession. When viewed from the perspective of the phenomenal reality, succession of universal consciousness is time, from the context of universal consciousness, succession is not just time, but it is "creative time, the potential for the emergent reality of emanation" (Rastogi 14).

This idea is best represented by the description of empirical reality as the play of consciousness. The need to play is intrinsic to reality—the play here means nature's tendency to create meaningful order out of diverse phenomena marked by creativity and novelty. The play is called *lila* because we arise from this flux, create our own pattern, and dissolve in the flux. The role of liberation then is the realization that the true nature of reality lies in its flowering or becoming. The description of reality as the *tandava* dance of Shiva beautifully illustrates the process of becoming and hints at its creative and aesthetic elements. The *Shivasutras* say: "The Self is the actor or the dancer [*nartaka atma*]" (SS 113). A good actor is sensitive to the emotive states (*rasa*) of the play and identifies completely with the part that she plays and yet in between the scenes, she reverts back to her own self and rejoices in the play of creation. Similarly, the Self within the self acts out its world drama through the activity of the senses, taking delight in its unfolding which is marked by spontaneity. According to the *Spandakarikas* "the realization of the liberated condition is the achievement of a state of pure enjoying subjectivity (*bhoktrta*), through which perfect mastery of every power is acquired...The liberated yogi thus conforms to S[h]iva's state which, beyond the opposites of subject and object, pleasure and pain, is the subject who enjoys the cosmic sport of the cycle of His universal manifestation" (Dyczkowski, SA 186).

Both the Self and the self are intricately intertwined. No eternity exists apart from temporal existence—one is enfolded in the other and does not exist apart from the other. The whole concept of eternity is usually abstracted from this complete description of reality. Even in interpretations of Shaiva texts where the emphasis has been on the dynamic aspects of reality, there is a strong tendency to abstract Shiva consciousness from the total description and regard it as existing separate in itself—giving it the place of an eternal God. Though Shiva and Shakti are often portrayed as a duality and sometimes even set in a conflictual stance, a close reading of the Kashmiri Shaiva texts reveals that Shiva/Shakti are not opposites. Shiva consciousness, therefore, cannot be abstracted from the total reality and seen as a separate entity. Instead, Shiva and Shakti are two aspects of the same indeterminate reality. "The motion of absolute consciousness is a creative movement, a transition from the uncreated state of Being to the created state of Becoming. In this sense Being is in a state of perpetual Becoming (*satatodita*); it constantly phenomenalises into finite expression" (Dyczkowski 1987, 77).

Perhaps we can understand this concept better if we refer to recent discoveries in quantum mechanics which cannot be explained on the basis of categories of human understanding and normal sense perceptions. At the quantum level the subatomic particles appear as both waves and particles. If instruments were used to describe their position, they register as particles and if their momentum was measured, they appear as waves. Each by itself is thus an incomplete description of the subatomic reality. Both the wave and particle descriptions are needed to give the complete picture. More fundamentally, reality is potential. By exercising our awareness in different ways we reduce the many possibilities to specific actuality. In this view, the evolution of outer reality is contingent on the groundstuff of consciousness. The well known quantum physicist David Bohm proposes a theory of reality based on his synthesis of insights into quantum reality with Eastern philosophical ideas. Bohm theorizes that there is an implicate order that is enfolded in the entire universe, a level where all of us are interconnected and a part of the whole making it possible for us to know the world. Things, entities, objects arise from this order, manifest, and vanish into it. Bohm uses the metaphor of a stream with its ripples, vortices, and splashes. As we experience a vortex, we tend to abstract it from the flow of the stream and describe it as independent of it. But the vortex does not exist independent of the flow and hence, its reality cannot be seen apart from the flow of the stream (Bohm, 1980). The commonly used analogy in Kashmiri Shaivite texts is to describe the relationship between the Shiva and Shakti or the Self and the self as that between the ocean and waves.

Becoming and not being then is the basis of reality. A Shaivite would say reality is the play of consciousness, and a physicist metaphysician might say reality is process—a flow of processes that are novel, creative, and evolving. Everything is part of the flux of this everchanging reality. If we were to use the metaphor of the ocean and the waves, one could say the individual is the wave and the ocean is Shiva. Just as the ocean is part of the reality of the wave, so it is with the Shiva consciousness that is the essential ground of the reality of empirical consciousness. As Abhinava says, the light of consciousness is the ground of both the subjective as well as the objective reality. From this perspective, it is senseless to talk about nature as simply dead and outside the domain of universal consciousness, since at the subatomic level both the living and nonliving entities are made of pure energy which is in dynamic flux. The fact that perception is possible demands that there be a common ground for the subjective as well as objective reality. The ultimate reality is the substratum of the diverse phenomenal world, starting from humans at the top of the evolutionary ladder down to the simplest non-living matter.

To bring out the relevance of Lalla's poetry for contemporary society, it is important to emphasize that Kashmir Shaivism that permeates her verses does not promote renunciation of the world. The *Spandakarikas* describe the relationship of the Self and the world as that between the mirror and its reflection. The reflection is not something separate from the mirror just as the created world is not separate from the Self. However, unlike the reflection which is of an object outside the mirror, there is nothing outside the consciousness that gets reflected. This is an important distinction which illustrates that the relationship between the consciousness and the empirical world is not based on positing the world as the other, outside of itself, and thereby assigning it a different order of reality. Instead, the empirical world exists within the mirror of consciousness and hence, the two are integrally related. The world is not a negative image of the Self, but it is an expression of the Self. In order to experience the Self, one need not negate the world but live it fully and completely. Yet in Lalla's verses in spite of their Shaiva content, there is an undue stress on the mirror part of this metaphor, and it is a mirror that does not reflect the world. The light of consciousness that illumines her inner reality bounces off the social structures of her material reality. Lalla's dancing is not the dancing of Shiva taking delight in its creation. Her life experiences in fact deconstruct the metaphor of dance—she symbolically derobes and divests herself of the body that would enable her to enjoy the dance. For her, the world is indeed *maya*, which hinders rather than helps her enjoy her insights into reality.

Lalla's Verses

transcribed and translated from the Kashmiri

1

ayes vate gayes na vate
sumana svathi manz lustum doh
candas vuchum ta har na athe
nav taras dim kya ba

My path to this world was direct
But my road back is not
The day passed by the riverside
Not a penny is in my pocket
What would I pay for being ferried across

2

ami pana sodaras navi chyes laman
kati bozi daya myon myeti diyi tar
amyen takyen poni zan shaman
zuv chum braman gara gatshaha

I pull the boat with untwisted yarn
Will God hear and help me across
Water leaks from unbaked clay saucers
My heart desires to go home

3

hachivi harinji petsiv kan gom
abakh chan pyom yath razdhane
manzbag bazaras kulfa rust van gom
tirtha rost pan gom kus mali zane

Like a grass arrow fitted on a wooden bow I am
My palace is in the hands of an ignorant carpenter
In the midst of the market place I am
like a shop without a lock
My body has become bereft of sanctity
Who would understand my plight [1]

4

nabadi baras ata gand dyol gom
deh kan hol gom hyeka kahyo
gora sund vanun ravan tyol pyom
pahali rost khyol gom hyeka kahyo

Loosened is the shoulder knot of
my candy load
Bent like a bow is my body
How can I carry this burden?
My guru's words to achieve detachment
are painful
Like a flock without a shepherd am I
How can I carry this burden?

[1] Lalla uses "grass arrow," "ignorant carpenter," and "shop without a lock" as metaphors to represent her novice self that has yet to develop powers of concentration and meditation.

5

gatulah akh vuchum bochi sity maran
pan zan haran puhani vav lah
nyashbod akh vuchum vazas maran
tan lal ba praran tshyenyem na prah

A wise one I saw dying of hunger
just as leaves fall with the early winter wind
I saw a fool beating his cook
Since then I, Lalla, am waiting for the moment
when my worldly ties are severed

6

kyah kara pantsan dahan ta kahan
vokhshun yath lyeji karith yim gaiy
sariy samahan yith razi lamahan
ada kyazi ravihe kahan gav

What will I do with the five, ten, and eleven
They have all emptied out the cauldron
If all had come together and pulled the rope
Then the eleven would not have lost the cow[2]

[2] The "cauldron" in this verse represents the physical body. The number "five" stands for five *bhutas* or principles of experiencing the physical world—solidity, liquidity, vacuity, formativity, and aeriality. The "ten" refers to the five sense organs along with the five organs of action, and the "eleven" refers to the previously mentioned ten organs and the mind. In this verse, Lalla seems to say that the world of senses pulls the attention outwards and scatters it in different directions. With the result, the experience of Shiva consciousness, here represented by the "cow" is lost. Also see Grierson, p. 108.

7

lalith lalith vaday ba vay
tsitta muhuc pyeyiy may
roziy no pata loh langaruc tshay
niza svaruph kya mothuy hay

I will gently lament for you
O mind, you are in love with illusions
Not a shadow of this worldly splendor will
accompany you
Oh, why do you forget your real nature

8

latan hund maz laryom vatan
akiy havnam akiciy vath
yim yim bozan tim kona matan
lali buz shatan kuniy kath

Soles of my feet wore off on different paths
Only One showed me the true path
Why do not those who hear it become enamored
Lalla heard only one word in a hundred words

9
paran paran zyev tal phajim
tsyeh yugi kriy tajim na zanh
sumran phiran nyoth ta anguj gajim
manach duyi mali tsajim na zanh

Continuous reading and reciting turned my tongue
and palate sore
Yet I did not find a practice appropriate for you
Turning the rosary beads have worn out my thumb
and finger
Yet my mind's confusion, my dear, did not leave me

10
ayes kami dishi ta kami vate
gatsha kami dishi kava zana vath
anti day lagimay tate
chyenis phvakas kantsh ti no sath

From which direction did I come and what road
did I take
Which direction shall I take? How will I know the path?
Finally the right guidance will come to my aid
Empty breath has no value [3]

[3] In Verse 8, 9, and 10, Lalla refers to her experimentation with different techniques in her spiritual quest. Reading religious scriptures as well as recitation of prayers and mantras prove fruitless. The only true path, she finally realizes, is to learn breath control which is the fundamental practice of meditation in the Kashmiri Shaiva tradition.

11

lal ba lusas tshandan ta gvaran
hal me koramas rasani shyetiy
vuchun hyotamas tarya dithimas baran
myeti kal ganyeyi ta zogamas tatiy

I, Lalla, became exhausted searching eagerly
I put more effort into it than I was capable of
When I started seeing, I saw the doors bolted
My yearning increased and I kept a watch there

12

lal ba drayes lola re
tshandan lustum dyen kyoh rath
vuchum pandith panani gare
suy me rotamas nyechtur ta sath

Full of love I set out
Day and night I spent searching
In my own home I met the Pandit [4]
whom I caught and this became my
auspicious moment

[4] Pandit (learned brahman) refers to the Self which is the object of Lalla's quest.

13

lal ba drayes kapasi poshyece sutsiy
kadi ta duni karanam yutsiy lath
tuyi yeli kharinam zayiji tuyi
bovari vana gayam alanzay lath

I, Lalla, set out in the hope of blooming like a
cotton flower
Ginner and carder gave me hard blows
The female spinner spun me into fine yarn
In the weaver's shop I was stretched on the loom

14

dobi yeli chavanas dobi kani pyethay
saz ta saban matshanam yutsiy
sutsi yeli phirnam hani hani kantsiy
ada lali me pravum parma gath

The washerman then dashed me on a slab of stone
Rubbing me with much soap and washing soda
Then the tailor cut me into bits with scissors
And only then I, Lalla, attained supreme bliss[5]

[5] Lalla describes in this and the preceding verse her arrival into the world full of potential, but the ginners, carders, spinners, and weavers of society have socialized her into a gendered self to serve purely utilitarian purposes. Lalla metaphorically expresses her deconditioning from this socialized role when her social self is washed clean and cut into bits in the hands of the washerman and the tailor which in this context represent Lalla's own higher Self yearning for knowledge.

15

goran vonunam kunuy vatsun
nyebra dopnam andray atsun
suy gauv lali me vakh ta vatsun
tavay me hyotum nangay natsun

My guru gave me only one advice—
From outside transfer the attention within
That became my initiation
That is why I began to wander naked [6]

16

goras pritshom sasi late
yas na kenh vanan tas kya nav
pritshan pritshan thacis ta lusas
kenh nas nishe kyah tam drav

Again and again I asked my guru
What is the name of the undefinable
Repeated questioning tired and exhausted me
Something has come out of this nothing [7]

[6] Lalla's reference to wandering in a nude state could signify her divesting or derobing herself of all worldly attachments, including her family, friends, and the comfort of a home.

[7] "Something" refers to the manifest world that has arisen from the "undefinable" and "unmanifest" reality, which sometimes is also called "nothingness" in the esoteric literature.

17

tshandan lusus pani panas
tshapith jnanas votum na kunh
lay karmas ta vatsas althanas
bari bari bana ta cyevan na kunh

Arduous was my search for the Self
Nothing compares to the hidden knowledge
Self-absorption led me to the house of nectar
Cups I found filled to the brim but nobody
was drinking

18

mal wondi zolum
jigar morum
tyeli lal nav dram
yeli dali travimas tatiy

Impurities of the heart I burned
Desires I killed
Lalla, my name, shone only
When I surrendered completely

19

yimay she tse timay she me
shyama-gala tse vyen tathis
yuhuy byen abheda tse te me
tsa shyen svami ba shyeyi mushis

You have six attributes and so do I
O, Blue-throated One [8] , without you I am afflicted
The difference between you and me—
You are the master of six whereas I am deluded
by them [9]

20

shiv va kishav va zin va
kamalaza nath nam darin yuh
me abali kasitan bhava raz
su va su va su va suh

The Self may be named Shiva, Keshava,
or Mahavir
Or the lotus born Buddha
Whatever name it may have
May it remove worldly attachments of
a weakling like me

[8] Shiva is also called the "Blue-throated One" in the mythological literature.

[9] The six attributes are anger, bewilderment, arrogance, passion, jealousy, and avarice. Lalla has yet to reach the level of detachment that would help her master the six attributes.

21

zanam pravith vyabhav na tshondum
luban bhugan bharam na priy
somuy ahar setha zonum
tsolum dvakh vav polum day

In life I did not desire affluence
Nor did I love greed or enjoyment of luxuries
Moderate meals I considered sufficient for me
I endured suffering and poverty and remained
devoted to God.

22

natha na pan na par zonum
saday gorum yekuy deh
tsa ba ba tsa myul no zonum
tsa kus ba kossa chu sandeh

O, Lord! the Self in myself and others I did
not recognize
I have always known only this body [10]
You and I are joined in one—I did not know
My doubts remained concerning who you are
and who I am.

[10] A variation of the second line reads "Continually I have mortified this vile body." See Grierson p. 28.

23

mandachi hankal kar tsenyem
yeli hyedun gelun asun prava
aruk jama karsana dazyem
yeli andryim kharyuk rozyem vara

The chain of embarrassment will only break
When I can tolerate taunts and mocking words
Robe of self-pity will burn away
When the inner unbridled horse [11] is brought
under control

24

rut ta krut soruy pazyem
kanan na bozun achin na bhava
oruk dapun yeli wondi vuzyem
ratandip prazalyem varzani vav

Both good and bad, I must endure
My ears don't hear, my eyes don't see
When the inner Self awakens in my heart
The lamp will shine even in the midst of a tornado [12]

[11] Lalla often uses the image of an "unbridled horse" to represent the scattered nature of restless mind that skips from thought to thought aimlessly and out of control.

[12] As Lalla proceeds on the path of renunciation, she encounters hardships and ridicule which she soon learns to bear with a sense of detachment. As her practice advances, she compares her experience to the lighting of an inner lamp which continues shining without wavering, even in the midst of the extreme hardships of her material existence.

25

lyeka ta thvaka pyeth sheri hyetsam
nyanda sapanim pat bronth tani
lal chas kal zanh no tshenim
ada yeli sapanis vyepihey kyah

I endured verbal abuse as well as slander
Scandals broke out about my past and present
I am Lalla and my yearning never stopped
When I achieved my goal, nothing affected me

26

tana mana gayes ba tas kuny
buzum satic ghanta vazan
tath jayi dharanay dharan ratam
akash ta prakash korum sarah

Physically and mentally I am absorbed in him
I heard the bell of truth ring
That is the state I meditated on
Then I realized the manifest and the unmanifest

27

kuneray bozakh kuni no rozakh
kuniran koranam haniyakar
kunuy asith dvan hund jang gom
suy berang gom karith rang

If you understand what non-duality is, you would
lose your "I-ness"
The realization of unity in duality has erased my
"I-ness"
In spite of being One, the conflict arising from
duality persists
The colorless One has dyed me in worldly colors.

28

loluk nar lali loli lalanovum
maranay mvayes ta ruzas na zaray
ranga ratshi zatsai kya na rang hovum
ba dapun tsalum kya sana karay

I, Lalla, suffered the fire of love
Before death I died without a trace
Born without color or creed, yet what colors didn't
I take "I-ness" left me
What else could I do?

29

ravana manzay ravun rovum
ravith athi ayas bhavasaray
asan gindan sahazay provum
dapanuy korum panas saray

In the midst of being lost, I lost the sense of being lost
After being lost I found myself in this worldly ocean
Laughing and playing, I attained all-pervading Self
This philosophy became a part of me [13]

30

pot zuni wothith mot bolanovum
dag lalanavum dayi sanzi prahe
lali lali karan lala vuzanovum
milith tas man shrotsyom dahe

Awakening in the early dawn
I summoned the restless mind
Enduring the pain I devoted myself to God
By saying "I am Lalla, I am Lalla," I awakened
my darling
By becoming one with Him, I purified
my mind and body

[13] Verse 28 and 29 refer to the material reality as colored by distinctions of all kinds. Lalla is born in this world where she takes many roles. When she begins her practice, she feels completely lost as she rejects socially and conventionally defined ways of experiencing and perceiving the world. However, she soon realizes that out of this experience of becoming lost emerges a deeper experience of finding herself as she realizes both the inner and the outer permeated by the same Shiva consciousness.

31

ye gora parameshvara
bavtam tse chuy antarvyod
doshevay wopadan kanda pura
huh kava tarun ta hah kava tot

O, Guru! you are Parameshvara to me
Reveal to me the inner truth that you know
Both *pranas* arise from the abode of navel *chakra*
Why is *huh* cold and *hah* hot [14]

32

nabisthanas chey prakryeth zalavani
hidis tam yeti pran wata-got
brahmanda pyetha suti nadi vahavani
huh tava turun ta hah tava tot

The region of the navel is naturally ablaze
The breath moves up to the throat
to the *brahmarandhra* from where the river flows
For this reason, *Huh* (inhaled breath) is cold
and *Hah* (exhaled breath) is hot

[14] In this and the next verse, Lalla refers to the meditation on the inhaled and the exhaled breath, which is a basic practice in Kashmir Shaivism.

33

dihaci lari dari bar troparim
prana tsur rotum ta dyutamas dam
hryedayici kuthari andar gondum
omaki cobaka tulamas bam

Doors and windows of my body I closed
My *prana*-thief I caught and brought under control
Then I tied it inside the chamber of my heart
And then I whipped it with the syllable Om [15]

34

tsitta turog vagi hyeth rotum
tsyalith milavith dashi nadi vav
tavay shashikal vyaglith vuchum
shunyes shunya milith gauv

I took the reins of the mind-horse
Through practice, I learned breath control
Then only the orb of moon melted and flowed
down into my body
Nothingness merged with nothingness

[15] This specific Kashmir Shaiva practice involves developing focused attention through disengaging oneself from sensory perceptions, withdrawing within, and exercising breath control and silent absorption in the sound Om.

35

tsa na ba na dhyiy na dhyan
gauv panay sarva kriy mashith
anyou dyuthukh kentsh na anvay
gay sath layi par pashith

Neither I or you nor the meditation or the object
of meditation exists
The all-doer forgets himself
The blind find this meaningless
The wise became one with this supreme state

36

andar asith nyebar tshondum
pavanan ragan karnam sath
dhyana kini day zagi kival zonum
rang gav sangas milith kyeth

Though within, I searched outside
The control of breath soothed my inner channels
Through meditation, I realized that God and the
world are one
The manifest world became merged with the
unmanifest

37

samsaras ayes tapasiy
bodha prakash lobum sahaz
maryem na kunh ta mara na kansi
mara nech ta lasa nech

As a hermit I came to this world
Through meditation on the Self,
    I attained realization
No one will die to me, and I will die
    to nobody
Death and life are the same

38

dvadashanta mandal yes divas thaji
nasika pavana dori anahata rav
svayam kalpan antihi tsaji
panay su div ta artsun kas

He who realized *brahmarandhra mandala*
    as the abode of the deity
And heard the all-pervasive unobstructed sound
    through breath control
And who erased the illusions about himself,
As he himself is the deity, then to whom should
    he worship

39

turi salil khota tay ture
himi tre gay byen abyen vimarsha
tsaitanyi rav bati sab same
shivamay tsaratsar zag pashya

Cold changes water into ice or snow
Discernment shows the three states though
    different are not really different
When the sun of consciousness shines,
The plurality is dissolved into oneness
Then the universe appears throughout
    permeated with Shiva

40

lub marun sahaz vyetsarun
droga zanun kalpan trav
nishi chuy ta dura mo garun
shunyes shunyah milith gauv

Abandon desires and meditate on the Self
Realization is hard to achieve, so stop
    daydreaming
It is near, so don't search afar
Nothingness merges with Nothingness

41

tanthar gali tay manthar mvatse
manthar gol tay motuy tsyeth
tsyeth gol tay kenh ti na kune
shunyes shunyah milith gauv

When teachings disappear, the mantra remains
When the mantra disappears, consciousness remains
When consciousness disappears, nothing remains
Nothingness merges with nothingness

42

she van tsatith shashikal vuzum
prakrath hunzum pavana satiy
lolaki nara valinj buzum
shankar lobum tamiy satiy

After traversing six forests, I awakened the orb
 of the moon [16]
By controlling my breath, I gave up attachment
 to worldly things
I burned my heart in the fire of love
Thus I found Shankar

[16] In Verse 42 and 43 "six paths" refers to six *chakras* or energy centers along the spine—*muladhara, svadhisthana, manipura, anahata, vishuddha, ajna*. The orb of moon is the seventh *chakra* or *brahmarandhra*. See page 81.

43

omkar yeli layi onum
vuhi korum panun pan
she vat travith ta sath marg rotum
tyeli lal ba vatsas prakashsthan

I became absorbed in the sacred syllable Om
I burned myself like coal
After traversing six paths, I seized the seventh
Then only did I, Lalla, reach the abode of light

44

ban gol tay prakash av zune
tsandar gol tay motuy tsyeth
cyeth gol tay kenh ti na kune
gay bhur bhuvah svar vyesarzith kyeth

The sun sets, the moon shines
The moon vanishes, consciousness remains
Consciousness disappears, then nothingness remains
And the physical, spiritual, and metaphysical merge
into nothingness

45
shiv gora tay keshav palanas
brahma payiren wolasyes
yogi yoga kali parzanyes
kus div ashvavar pyeth cedyas

Shiva is the horse and Vishnu is the saddle
And Brahma is on the stirrups
A yogi through yogic practice recognizes the One
Who is riding on this horse

46
anahath kha svaruph shunyalay
yes nav na varan na guthar ta ruph
aham vimarshye nad binduy yes von
suy div ashvavar pyeth cedyes

The unstruck sound of Om
All permeating, whose abode is void
With no name, no color, no caste, no form
Self-introspection reveals it as the unsounded
resonance
That is the deity who rides the horse

47

dami dithim nad vahavaniy
dami dyuthum sum na ta tar
dami dithim thara phvalavaniy
dami dyuthum gul na ta khar

Just now I saw a flowing river
And then I saw a vast expanse of water without a
bridge or a ferry
Just now I saw a shrub with blossoming flowers
And then I saw neither flowers nor thorns[17]

48

dami dithim gaj dazvaniy
dami dyuthum dah na ta nar
damiy dithim pandavan hunz maji
dami dithim krajiy mas

Just now I saw fire ablaze in the hearth
And then I saw neither the smoke nor fire
Just now I saw the mother of Pandavas
And then I saw her as the aunt in the potter's house

[17] Verses 47, 48, and 49 illustrate the ephemeral nature of the phenomenal world. Lalla imagines herself outside time as she surveys the coming into existence and disappearance into nothingness of the objects and processes of the material world. The "flowing river," the "lake," the "shrub with blossoming flowers, the "fire ablaze in the hearth" all come and go. In Verse 48, Lalla makes reference to the epic *Mahabharata* in which the Pandava brothers are obliged to go into hiding after their lac-house burns down. For some time they live at a potter's house in Kampilya where Kunti is introduced to others as the potter's aunt. It is soon after this episode that the brothers go to Draupadi's *svyamvara* and win her.

49

trayi nyengi sarah sari saras
aki nyengi saras arshas jay
harmvakha kausara akh sum saras
sati nyengi saras shunyakar

Three times I saw the lake overflowing
Once I saw a place to step on in the sky
Once I saw a bridge from Harmukh to Kausar
Seven times I saw the manifest world vanish
in the void.

50

yih kyah asith yih kyuth rang gom
cang gom tsatith huda hudenyey dagay
sariniy padan kunuy vakhum pyom
lali me trag gom laga kami shathay

What was I and what has become of me
My attachments have been severed
All the verses echo only one thing
I, Lalla, have become a lake
Where shall I find my shore [18]

[18] See Grierson, p.99. The words *huda hudanyey* in the original Kashmiri verse are obscure and, hence, the translation of the second line in Verse 50 (Grierson Verse 84) is incomplete.

51

yih kyah asith yih kyuth rang gom
berang karith gom lag kami shathay
talav razadane abakh chan pyom
jan gom zanyem pan panunuy

What was I and what has become of me
I became colorless, where shall I find my shore
The top of the palace has an ignorant carpenter
It was good for me, I understood my own self[19]

52

parun svalabh palun dvarlabh
sahaz garun sukshm ta kruth
abhyaski ghaniray shastr muthum
tsetan anand niscay gom

Easy to read but difficult to follow
Attaining self-knowledge is subtle and difficult
Absorbed in practice, I forgot the scriptures
Consciousness-bliss I realized

[19] Both Verse 50 and 51 have the same first line. It is possible that the first line of the verse was lost and eventually replaced by the line from the previous verse. Thus, we have two verses here with the same first line—though in Verse 51, the first line does not flow with the second line and the third does not flow with the thought content of the fourth line. To have color in Lalla's verses means to define oneself through the material and social milieu in which one lives that includes caste, gender, class, and religion. Shiva, on the other hand, transcends these distinctions. Lalla's experience of herself as colorless means her realization of Shiva in herself and in the world around her. According to Grierson, the third line in the verse does not make sense and that could be because the word "abakh" is not used anymore. If the line is translated literally by using the meaning for a related word "abakhvaryeth" which means clumsy, Lalla's reference to "ignorant carpenter" could mean her inability to integrate her spiritual experience into her daily life. However, this meaning does not go with what comes before and after.

53

parum polum apuruy purum
kesari vana volum ratith shal
paras prunum ta panas polum
ada gom molum ta zinim hal

What I read, I followed, the unreadable I got
    through direct experience
I brought down the lion from the forest like a jackal
My teachings for others, I followed myself
Only then I attained knowledge and achieved my goal [20]

54

dishi ayes dash dishi tilith
tsalith tsotum shuny ada vav
shivay dyuthum shayi shayi milith
she ta tre tropimas ta shivay drav

After wandering in ten directions, I found
    the true path
Through breath control, I penetrated the void
Shiva I saw permeating everywhere
When I shut the six and the three [21]
I found Shiva as the root cause of all

[20] The lion is a metaphor for desires that continually entangle humans in worldly affairs. The subduing of desires is represented by the transformation of the lion into the jackal. Lalla brings her desires under control and then only is she able to proceed on her quest and achieve her goal of self-realization.
[21] The "six" refers to the five sense organs and the mind, while the "three" are the three body openings. When Lalla directs her attention inward and brings the flow of sensory perceptions to a halt, she realizes that Shiva permeates both the inner and the outer world.

55

shunyuk maidan kodum panas
me lali ruzam na bvadh na hosh
bhediy sapanis panay panas
ada kami gili phol lali pamposh

I traversed the field of void alone
And I, Lalla, lost consciousness of myself
I found the secret of my Self
Then, the lotus bloomed in the mud for Lalla

56

mithya kapat asath trovum
manas korum suy wopadish
zanas andar kival zonum
anas khyanas kus chum dvish

Renouncing cheating, deceit, and hypocrisy
Is the teaching I told my mind to follow
Only One I found in every thing
Then what is wrong with eating with people from
different castes or religions

57
ayes ti syoduy ta gatsha ti syoduy
syadis hol me karyem kyah
ba tas asas agaray vyeday
vidis ta vyendis karyem kyah

I came here directly and I will return directly
What can wickedness do to my simple and
honest nature
I am known to the beginningless source
As its acquaintance and loved one, no harm
can come to me

58
lal ba tsayes svaman baga baras
vuchum shivas shakath milith ta vah
tati lay karam amrita saras
zinday maras ta me kari kyah

I, Lalla, entered the door to the garden of my mind
I saw Shiva and Shakti in communion
I became immersed in the nectar of bliss
I died while still alive
Nothing worries me

59

gagan tsay bhutal tsay
tsay chukh dyen pavan ta rath
arg tsandan posh poni tsay
tsay chukh soruy ta lagiziy kyah

You are the sky and you are the earth
You are the day, the night and the wind
You are the grain, sandalwood, flowers, and water
You are everything, then what should I offer to you

60

tsyeth novuy tsandarama novuy
zalamay dyuthum navam novuy
yena pyetha lali me tan man novuy
tana lal ba navam naviy chyes

The consciousness is new and the moon is new
I saw the whole universe moment by moment renewed
Ever since I, Lalla, cleansed my body and mind
I, Lalla, have become ever renewed

61

andariy ayes tsandariy garan
garan ayes hihyen hih
tsay he naran tsay he naran
tsay he naran yim kam vih

From within I came searching for the moon.[22]
I continued seeking similar symbols
You are Narayan; you are Narayana
You are Narayan—why these distinctions?

62

tsay diva gartas ta dhartiy srazak
tsay diva ditith kranzan pran
tsay diva thani rustuy vazak
kus zani diva con pariman

O God, you permeate the creation on the earth
O God, You give life to matter
O God, You resonate without sound
Who can fathom You?

[22] See page 81.

63

pavan purith yusa ani vagi
tas bana sparshi na bvachi ta tresh
ti yes karun antihi tagi
samsaras suy zyeyi nech

He who controls the inhaled breath,
Hunger or thirst does not touch him
Whoever does this until the end
Is born fortunate in the world

64

zanaha nadi dal man ratith
tsatith vatith kutith klish
zanaha ada asta rasayen gatith
shiv chuy kruth ta tsen wopadish

Had I known how to control the inner channels
How to cut them and how to bind them
I would have ended my suffering
Then I would have made the elixir
Shiva is difficult to attain, heed that advice

65

damah dam kormas daman hale
prazlyom diph ta nanyeyem zath
andryum prakash nyebar tshotum
gati rotum ta karmas thaph

Slowly through the practice of breath control
The lamp shone and I saw my true nature
Inner light I realized
Caught it in the darkness and seized it

66

gal gandinyem bol parinyem
dapinyem ti yes yih rotse
sahaza kusumav puz karinyem
ba amlany ta kas kya mvatse

Let them hurl abuses at me or lecture me
Let them call me what they wish
Let them offer me flowers of devotion
I am untouched, so what will they gain by it

67

lolaki wokhala walinj pishim
kvakal tsajim ta ruzas rasa
buzum ta zajim panas tsashim
kava zana tava sita mara kina lasa

I ground my heart in the mortar of love
Evil thoughts left me and I became calm
I burned and roasted the heart, and tasted it myself
How do I know if this practice will let me live or die

68

makuras zan mal tsalum manas
ada me labam zanas zan
suh yeli dyuthum nishi panas
soruy suy ta ba no kenh

Impurities from my mind were wiped away
like that from a mirror
Then only did I attain self-knowledge
I saw him near me
He is everything, and I am nothing

69

panas lagith rudukh me tsah
me tse tshandan lustum doh
panas manz yeli dyuthukh me tsah
me tse ta panas dyutum tshoh

When I was attached to the ego-consciousness
You remained hidden from me
Time passed in my search for you
When I saw you within
You and I were united in ecstasy

70

yi yi karm korum suh artsun
yi rasani wotsorum tiy manthar
yuhuy logamo dihas partsun
suy yi parama shivun tanthar

Deeds I performed became an offering
Words I spoke became mantra
Experiences my body had were for self-knowledge
This is the essence of the path of Shiva tantras

71

shiva shiva karan hamsa gath svarith
ruzith vyevahari dyan kyoh rath
lagi rosti advaya yus man karith
tasi nyeth prasana suragoranath

Reciting the name of Shiva and meditating on *hamsa*
While conducting worldly activities day and night
Liberating one's mind from desires and duality
Such a person always pleases the lord of creation

72

kus dingi ta kus zagi
kus sar vatari teli
kus haras puzi lagi
kus parama pad meli

Who is asleep and who is awake?
What lake is that whose water oozes away?
What is that which can be offered to Hari in worship?
What supreme state is fit to be attained?

73
man dingi ta akval zagi
dadi sar panca yindi vatari teli
swa vyetsara pon haras puzi lagi
parama pad tsetana shiv meli

Mind is asleep, the nameless Self is awake
Five sense organs are the lake from which water
constantly oozes
Self introspection is the water to be offered to Shiva
Shiva consciousness is the supreme state to be achieved

74
kus push ta kvassa pushani
kam kusum lagizyes puze
kami god dizyes zalci dani
kava sana manthar shankar svatma vuze

Who is the male and the female florist?
Which flowers should be offered for worship?
Which water should be used for anointing?
Which mantra will awaken the Shankar within?

75

man pusha tay yatsh pushani
bhavaki kusum lagizyes puze
shashirasa god dizyes zalaci doni
tshvapi mantra shankar svatma vuze

Mind is the male and desire the female florist
Offer the flowers of devotion in worship
Anoint with the eternal nectar dripping from the moon
Silent recitation will awaken the Shankar within

76

ha tsetta kava chuy logmut paramas
kava goy apazis pazyuk bronth
dushi boz vash kornakh paradharmas
yina gatshana zyena maranas kront

O Mind! Why are you attached to the external world
Why do you mistake illusory for the real
Lack of wisdom has won you over to the wrong path
Resigned to coming and going, death and rebirth.

77

asa bol parinyem sasa
me mani vasa khid na hyeyi
ba yid sahaza shankara bhakts asa
makaris sasa mal kyah pyeye

Even if thousands of abuses are hurled at me
In my heart I am not hurt
I am a devotee of all-pervading Shankar
Ashes cannot soil the mirror

78

tala chuy zyus tay pyetha chuk natsan
vanta mali man kyetha patsan chuy
soruy sombrith yeti chuy mutsan
vant mali ann kyetha rotsan chuy

Below you a pit and above it you are dancing
Tell me, O, dear, how can you depend on it
Everything you accumulate will be left behind
Tell me, O, dear, how can you enjoy your repast

79

atshyen ay ta gatshun gatshe
pakun gatshe dyen kyoh rath
yoray ay ta turi gatshun gatshe
kenh na ta kenh na ta kenh na ta kyah

Birth and death continue uninterruptedly
As long as day and night come and go
From where we came that is where we must return
What is there in it if not something

80

yuh yi karam kari pyetarun panas
arzun barzun byeyis kyut
antihi lagi rost pushyerun svatmas
ada yuri gatsha ta turi chum hyot

Responsibility for one's actions one must bear
Others share their fruits
Without attachment, I offer my actions to the Self
So wherever I go, it is good for me

81

sahazas sham ta dam no gatshi
yitshi no pravakh mukti dvar
salilas lavan zan milith gatshi
toti chuy durlab sahaza vyetsar

For self-knowledge, you don't just need
self-restraint and breath control
Liberation you will not achieve through wishing alone
Even though you are completely absorbed in the
Self like salt is dissolved in water
Then also it is rare to know the truth about the Self

82

asiy asi tay asiy asau
asiy dor kari patavat
shivas sori na zyun ta marun
ravas sori na atagat

In the past we existed and in the future we shall be
Through the ages we have been
Shiva continues with creation and dissolution
Just as the sun continues to rise and set

83

shiv chuy thali thali rozan
mo zan hyond ta musalman
truk ay chukh ta pan panun parzanav
svay chay sahibas sitya zaniy zan

Shiva is omnipresent
Don't differentiate between Hindus and Muslims[23]
If you are wise, you will recognize your true self.
That is your real acquaintance with the Lord

84

kush posh tel diph zal na gatshe
sadbhava gora kath yusa mani hyeye
shambhus svari nityi panani yitshe
sada pyeze sahaza kriy na zyaye

No need for kusha grass, flowers, sesame seeds, lamp,
  or water
Whosoever accepts the teacher's word in simple faith,
And remembers Shambhu daily of his own volition,
Always absorbed in all-pervasive unobstructed sound
  becomes liberated

[23] In the original verse, the word "hyond" seems to be a later addition as we don't come across the word "hindu" in Jonaraja's *Rajatarangini* where "brahmin" is frequently used for signifying Hindus. The word "musulman" is a local variation of the term "Mausula" that seems to be the term used to refer to Muslims in medieval Kashmir as we come across it in both Jonaraja's and Shrivara's texts which were written in the fifteenth century. The word "sahib" in the original verse reflects Persian influence and seems to be a later addition.

85

abhyasi savikas layi wothu
gaganas sagun myula sami tsrata
shunya gol ta anamay mvatu
yuhuy wopadish chuy bata

Through constant practice the objective reality
is withdrawn
The world of forms and colors suddenly merges
with void
When the void disappears nameless consciousness
remains
This is my teaching, O Pandit! [24]

86

vakh manas kval akval na ate
tshvapi mudri ati na pravesh
rozan shiva shakath na ate
motayai kunh ta suy wopadish

Speech or mind, manifest or transcendental have
no existence there
Yogic silence has no place there
Shiva and Shakti don't live there
Seek whatever is left beyond it, this is your lesson

[24] In the original verse, the term "bata" refers to Kashmiri brahmins or Pandits. We come across the term "bhatta" both in Jonaraja's and Shrivara's texts where it is used to refer to Kashmiri brahmins.

87

mudo kriy chey na dharun ta parun
mudo kriy chey na rachin kay
mudo kriy chey na dih sandarun
sahaz vetsarun chuy wopadish

O, Foolish One, the right action is not observing
 fasts and rituals
And it is not protecting your body
Right action is not maintaining your body
Meditation on the Self is the teaching you should follow

88

prathuy tirthan gatshan sanyasi
gvaran svadarshana myul
tsitta parith mo nishpath as
deshakh dure dramun nyul

A religious mendicant goes to every holy place
Seeking to attain self-knowledge
O, mind, in spite of learning do not be directionless
From a distance the grass looks greener

89
tsyeth turog gagani bramavon
nimishi aki tshandi yuzana lach
tsetani vagi bvadhi ratith zon
pran apan sandarith pakhach

The mind-horse wanders all over
With the flicker of an eyelid, it travels a hundred
thousand leagues
She who holds the reins with self-restraint
and discrimination
Succeeds in controlling the inhaled and exhaled breath

90
shishiras vuth kus ratey
kus bvakey ratey vav
yus pants yindrey tsyelith tsetey
suy ratey ghatey rav

Who can stop the drip from icicles?
Who can hold air in the palm?
She who controls the five sense organs
Sees the sun in the darkness

91

laz kasey shit nivarey
tran zal karey ahar
yi kami wopadish koruy huta bata
atsitan vatas sutsitan kath dyun ahar

It covers your body and protects you from cold.
It lives on grass and water
Who gave you the advice, foolish Pandit,
To give lifeless stones the offering of a living creature

92

tsala tsitta wondas bhayi mo bar
tsyon tsinth karan pan anad
tse ko zanani khsod hari kar
kiwal tasunduy taruk nad

O, fickle mind! Don't let your heart be overcome by fear
The Beginningless itself looks after you
You do not know when your hunger will be satiated
Meditate on the all-permeating unobstructed sound alone

93

atha ma ba travun khar ba
luka hunz kvang var khyeyiy
tati kus ba dariy thar ba
yeti nanis kartal pyeyiy

Don't let the donkey get loose
It will graze the saffron fields of other people
Who will take the punishment for you
When exposed, you will be attacked by the sword [25]

94

jnanki ambar pairith tane
yim pad lali dapi tim hryedi ankh
karnay pranavaki lay kor lale
tsyeth jyoti kasan maranuni shankh

Wear the clothes of wisdom
Inscribe Lalla's verses on your heart
Through *pranava* Lalla became absorbed in the
light of consciousness [26]
Thereby she overcame the fear of death.

[25] This verse metaphorically describes the human condition. When the mind is allowed to wander aimlessly, it becomes preoccupied with worldly things which leave marks on both the spiritual and physical body. We alone are responsible for our actions and must bear responsibility for them.

[26] *Pranava* involves meditation on the syllable Om.

95

par tay pan yemi som mon
yemi hyuv mon dyen kyoh rath
yemisay advay man sonpun
tamiy dyuthuy suragoranath

Whosoever regards the self and the other as equal
And the day and night as the same
Whose mind is free of duality
She alone has the vision of lord of creation.

96

avitsari pothyen chi ho mali paran
yith tota paran 'rama' pinjaras
gita paran ta hitha laban
param gita ta paran chyas

Without discernment, O, dear, they read religious books
As parrots recite 'Rama" in a cage
Reading the Gita becomes an excuse
I have read the Gita and I am still reading it

97

kava chukh divan aniney batsh
trukh ay chukh ta andray atsh
shiva chuy ati tay kun mo gatsh
sahaza kathi myani karto patsh

Why are you groping like the blind
If you are wise, you will turn your attention within
Shiva is there, you need not go anywhere else
Believe my simple words

98

zanani zayay rati tay katiy
karith wodaras bahu klish
phirith dvar bazani vati tatiy
shiv chuy kruth ta tsen wopadish

We are born to the mother healthy and fit
After causing much suffering to her when inside the womb
Then we return and wait for the same door
It is hard to attain Shiva—keep that teaching in mind.

99

yosay shel pithas ta paṭas
svay shel chey prathivun dish
svay shel shubavanis gratas
shiv chuy kruth ta tsen wopadish

The stone that is on the pedestal and upon the
pavement
Is the same stone that comes from the earth
The same stone adorns the grindstone
It is hard to attain Shiva—keep that teaching in mind[27]

100

rav mata thali thali taptitan
tapitan wottam wottam dish
varun mata luka gara atsitan
shiv chuy kruth tay tsen wopadish

Will the sun not shine everywhere
Instead of shining only on good places?
Will the rain god Varuna refrain from entering
every house?
Attaining Shiva is difficult, remember that teaching[28]

[27] All stones come from the same earthly source irrespective of the function they serve. Lalla says, humans, too, though they belong to different castes, creeds, and classes, come from the same source.

[28] In this verse, too, Lalla assures the common people of different castes, classes, and creeds that all of them are equally capable of acquiring self knowledge since Shiva permeates both the inner and outer reality. Just as the sun shines and the rain falls on both good and bad places equally, so it is with people. Anyone who has will power and desire to achieve self-knowledge can realize it.

101

asi pvandi zvasi zami
nyethay snan kari tirthan
vahri vahras nonuy asi
nishi chuy ta parzantan

Laughing, sneezing, coughing, and yawning
Bathing daily at holy places
Revealed throughout the year
It is near you, so recognize it

102

shiv chuy zavyul zal vaharavith
kranzan manz chuy tarith kyath
zinda nay vuchihan ada kati marith
pana manz pan kad vyatsarith kyath

Like a fine net spread everywhere is Shiva
Subtly permeating the physical manifestation
If you don't see him when you are alive,
how can you do it when you are dead?
Through self-introspection get rid of the self
in yourself

103

yihay matri rupi pay diye
yihay bharya rupi kari vishish
yihay maya rupi anti zuv hyeye
shiv chuy kruth ta tsen wopadish

As mother she suckles the child
As wife she performs yet another role
In the end she takes the life away in the form of illusion
To attain Shiva is difficult, keep that teaching in mind [29]

104

kandyev grih tyezi kandyev van vas
vyephola man na ratith ta was
dyan rath ganzarith panun shvas
yuthuy chukh ta tyuthuy as

Some renounce their home and some their hermitage
All this is futile if the mind is not brought under control
Meditate on your breath day and night
And stay where you are

[29] Lalla refers to women's different roles as symbolized by Shakti who in her diverse manifestations brings the phenomenal world into existence. It is, finally, Shakti again, she says, who by withdrawing into Shiva brings the world to an end.

105

rangas manz chuy byon byon labhun
soruy tsalakh barakh svakh
tsakh roosh ta vair ay galakh
ada deshakh shiva sund mvakh

The world is full of differences
If you are tolerant, you will be happy
You will end anger, hate, and animosity
Then only will you see Shiva's face

106

ha manashi kyazi chukh vuthan syeki lavar
ami rati ha mali pakiy na nav
lyukhuy yi narani karmani rikhi
ti mali hyekiy na phirith kanh

O, Fellow Being! Why are you twisting ropes of sand
By holding on to this rope, O dear, the boat will not move
Whatever Narayana has written in your karma
Nobody, O, dear, can change[30]

[30] The phrase "twisting ropes of sand" refers to futile efforts for achieving self-realization. The last two lines do not follow the thought expressed in the first two lines as it seems to point to human helplessness in the face of predetermined fate. Lalla, however, does not mean that our life is predetermined by a divine agency. Rather through motivated actions, both good and bad, we enmesh ourselves in the world where we must live out the fruits of our actions. Only through engaging in detached actions can we finally find liberation.

107

jnana marg cheyi haka var
dizyes sham dam kriyi pani
lamatsakra posh prany kriy dar
khyena khyena mvatsiy varuy cheniy

The path of wisdom is like a kitchen garden
Nurture it with self-restraint, tranquillity, and good deeds
Fruits of old deeds will be paid off like the animal
sacrificed to the goddess
Eating ceaselessly from the garden will turn it barren [31]

108

buthi kyah jan chuk wonda chuy kaniy
aslac kath zanh saniy no
paran lekhan vuth anguj gajiy
andrim duyi zanh tsajiy no

You have a charming face but a heart of stone
The truth never penetrated you
Reading and writing wore out your lips and fingers
But the inner confusion never left you

[31] Offering the fruits of actions to the Self and traversing the path of wisdom, Lalla says, will free people from the *karmic* bondage caused by motivational deeds that lead to attachment and further entanglement in the world. Following the path of wisdom consistently, according to Lalla, will one day empty the kitchen garden of *karmic* deeds.

109

tsarman tsatith ditith pani panas
tyuth kya wavyoth ta phalihiy sov
mudas wopadish gay rinzi dumatas
kani dandas gor aparith rov

After removing the skin, you have put walls all
around yourself
What did you sow to have produced this fruit?
Teaching a fool is like throwing pebbles at a dome
Or expecting to milk a brown bull after feeding it
with molasses [32]

110

mud zanith pashith ta kor
kol shrutavon zada rupi as
yus yi dapiy tas tiy bol
yuhuy tattva vidis chuh abhyas

Act ignorant, even if you know
Act blind, even if you see
Act deaf, even if you hear
In short, act emotionless
Whatever people tell you, listen and agree
This practice will lead to knowledge

[32] This verse seems to refer to Lalla's frustration in teaching esoteric ideas to those people who are totally submerged in the material world. She describes such people reducing themselves to their bodies (hide), stretching it and anchoring it in the material world through pegs of desire. As Jayalal Kaul points out, this vivid image of human hide tied to the world through pegs of desire captures the image of a life that is cut off from any higher aspirations that could blossom into experiences of the Self in the self. "The best you can do with a hide is to dress it, tan it, stretch and polish it but you cannot bring the animal to life" (63).

111

tsalun chu vuzamala ta tratay
tsalun chu mendinyen gatakar
tsalun chu pan panun kadun gratay
hyeta mali santush vati panay

Learn to endure lightning and thunder
Learn to endure darkness at noon
Learn to endure passing through the grinding mill
If you are content, dear, he will come to you.

112

tyoth modur tay myuth zahr
yes yuth tshanukh jatanbhav
yemi yath kariy kal ta kahar
su tath shahar vatith pyev

Bitter is sweet and sweet is poisonous
The amount of effort
And single-minded devotion determines
the final achievement

113

div vata divar vata
pyetha bvana chuy yekavath
puz kas karakh hotha bata
kar manas ta pavanas sangath

The idol is stone, the temple is stone
It is all one from top to bottom
Who will you worship, learned Pandit?
Learn to control your mind and your breath

114

mudas jnanach kath no vanizey
kharas gor dinah raviy doh
seki shathas phal no vavizey
ravrizih na kum yajan til

Don't talk to a fool about knowledge
Giving molasses to a donkey is a waste of time
Don't plant seeds in the sandy river bank
Don't waste oil over bran cakes [33]

[33] This verse appears as a eight line verse in Anand Koul collection (Verse 32 July 1930). The first two lines of each verse appear to be a later addition. Out of the eight line verse, I have taken four lines that follow the metaphoric style of Lalla's verses.

115

yeva turi tsali tim ambar hyeta
khsod yeva gali tim ahar ann
tsitta sva para vyetsaras pyeta
tsitta dehas van kya van

Wear those clothes that protect you from cold
Eat that food which satisfies your hunger
Meditate on the Self
O, Mind! Give your body this advice

116

treshi bvachi mo kreshanavun
yani tshiy tani sandharun dih
phrit canis dharun ta parun
kar wopkarun suy chay kriy

Don't torture your body with thirst and starvation
When the body is exhausted, take care of it
Cursed be your fasts and religious ceremonies
Do good to others, for that is the real religious practice

117

khyena khyena karan kun no vatak
na khyena gachakh ahamkari
somuy kheh mali somuy asak
sami khyenah mutsaranay baranyen tari

Indulging in eating will lead you nowhere
By refraining from eating, you will become egotistical
By eating moderately, you will achieve equanimity
By practicing moderation, the closed doors will
be unbolted [34]

118

khyeth gandith shami na manas
branth yimav trav timay gay khasit
shastra buzith chuh yema bhayi krur
su na potṣa ta daniy lasith

Tranquillity is not achieved by eating and clothing oneself
Those who give up false hopes attain their goal
Listening to scriptures intensifies the fear of death.
He who does not lean on them flourishes

[34] This verse in Anand Koul collection, Oct 1931 has two additional lines *sum yeli samiy rum kati roziy/sa ha mali sapanak*—"*So'hm, suy*" which appear to be a later addition.

119

hyeth karith rajy pheri na
dith karith trupti na man
luba vyena ziv mari na
zivant mari tay suy chuy jnan

Acquiring a kingdom will not make you content
Renouncing it will not satisfy your mind
If free from desires, you will not die
Self-knowledge is to be dead to worldly things while
still alive

120

kus mari ta kasu maran
mari kus tay maran kas
yus hara hara travith ghara ghara kare
ada su mari tay maran tas

Who will die and who will be killed?
Who will it kill and who will kill it?
Who instead of chanting "hara," "hara" recites
"gara," "gara"[35]
is the one who dies and the one who is killed

[35] "Hara" is a term commonly used to refer to Vishnu and "gara" means "home" in Kashmiri. In this verse, however, chanting "gara" refers to one's preoccupation with worldly affairs.

121
gora shabdas yus yatsh patsh bharey
jnana vagi rati tsyeta turgas
yindrey shumrith anand karey
ada kus mari tay maran kas

Whoever trusts the guru's words
Seizes the mind-horse with the reins of knowledge
And controlling the senses, attains bliss
Then who will die and who will be killed?

122
shil ta man chuy pon kranje
mvatsi yemi rot malli yod vav
hosta yus mast vala gande
ti yes tagi tay su ada nihal

Name and fame is like water in a sieve
Whoever has the strength to hold air in a fist
and who can tie an elephant with a strand of hair,
he is the one who will certainly attain bliss

123

zal thamavun hutavah turanavun
vurdhva gaman pairiv tsarith
katha dheni dvad shramnavun
antih sakali kapata tsarith

Stopping rain and extinguishing fire
Levitation
Milking a wooden cow—
In the end, all this is deceitful exhibition

124

yemi lubh manmath mad tsur morun
vata nashi marith ta logun das
tamiy sahaz ishvar gorun
tamiy soruy vyondun svas

Whoever kills greed, lust, and ego
And then serves people with humility
She yearns for all pervading Ishvar
And perceives everything around as ashes

125
rajyes baji yemi kartal tyaji
svargas baji chuy taph tay dan
sahazas baji yemi gora kath paji
papa pvani baji chuy panunuy pan

He who is a skilled swordsman acquires a kingdom
He who engages in penance and charity goes to heaven
He who follows the guru's words gains self-knowledge
He himself reaps the fruit of his good and bad deeds

126
okuy omkar yus nabhi dare
kumbuy brahmandas sum gare
akh suy manthar tsyetas kare
tas sas manthar kyah kare

She who holds an Om in the navel
And through breath control raises it
to *brahmarandhra*
And is absorbed in only this mantra
She has no need for other mantras

127

marukh mara buth kam krudh lubh
na ta kan barith mariney pan
manay khyen dikh svavyetsara shyem
vishey tihund kyah kyuth dora zan

Kill your mortal enemies—lust, anger, and desire
Otherwise they would kill you with their arrows
Calm them with self-restraint and good thoughts
Recognize their nature and their power

128

kalan kala zali yodwai tse gol
vyendiv gih va vyendiv vanvas
zanith sarvagath prabhu amol
yuthuy zanyekh tyuthuy as

With time as your longings disappear
Whether you are a householder or a recluse
You realize prabhu as pure and all pervading
Just what you perceive is what you will attain

129
tsidanandas jnana prakashyes
yimav tsyun tim zivanti mukht
vishamis samsaranis pashyes
abodh gandah shyeth shyeti ditiy

Those who achieve light-consciousness-bliss
Are alone liberated while alive
Tangled in the net of worldly existence
Ignorant people tie hundreds of knots

130
kenh chiy nyendri hatiy vudiy
kentsan wodyen nyesar pyeyi
kenh chiy snan karith aputiy
kenh chiy gih bazith ti akriy

Some though asleep are awake
Some while awake have fallen asleep
Some are dirty after a bath
And some even as householders are totally detached

131

grata chuh pheran zerey zerey
uhukuy zani gratuk tshal
grata yeli pheri tay zavyul nerey
gu vati panay gratabal

The grindstone moves when it is set in motion
Only the axle knows the mystery of the grindstone
When the grindstone moves, then only we get fine flour
And the wheat moves automatically in the grindstone
to be crushed [36]

132

yeth saras siriphol na vyetsiy
tath sari sakaliy poni tsyen
mrag srugal gandi zala hastiy
zyen na zyen ta totuy pyen

All drink from the lake
which cannot hold a grain of mustard
Deer, jackals, rhinoceros, and hippopotamus
All arising from it, instantly fall into it [37]

[36] The grindstone grinding flour becomes a metaphor for human life itself. If The grindstone represents the empirical self, then the axle is the Self which runs the grindstone. Only steady rotation of the axle produces finely ground flour. Lalla thus says that steady practice and focused meditation on the Self will ultimately lead to self-knowledge.

[37] The lake is a metaphor for ultimate reality which is beyond spatiotemporal dimensions and is the source of the manifest world. Seen from the perspective of this ultimate reality, the manifest world is just an instant flash that comes into existence and vanishes away.

133
azapa gayatri hamsa hamsa zapith
aham travith suy ada rath
yemi trov aham su rud panay
ba na asun chuy wopadish

Recite *So'ham* with every breath
Renounce the ego and meditate on the Self
She who renounces the ego finds the Self
Negation of the ego or "I" is the teaching

134
woth rainya artsun sakhar
athi alpal vakhur hyeth
yodavanay zanakh parama pad akhyer
hishiy khvashi khvar kyetha khyeth

Arise, Lady! Prepare for worship
With wine, meat, and a dainty choice of food
If you know the supreme state
Breaking customs will make no difference

135

marith pants buth tim phal handi
tsetana dana vakhur khyeth
taday zanakh parama pad tsandi
hishiy khoshi khor koti na khyeth

Kill the five principles of experience[38] after
fattening them
On a diet of meditation
Then only will you realize the supreme syllable
Breaking customs will make no difference

136

dachinis ubras zayun zanaha
samudras zanaha kadith ath
mandis rogiyas vaidyut zanaha
mudas zanim na pranit kath

I might have known how to scatter
southern clouds
Dry up an ocean
Cure a chronically sick person
But I never knew how to convince a fool

[38] The *panchabhutas* are five principles of experience of the physical world. See p. 76.

137

kandyo karakh kanda kande
kandyo karakh kandi vilas
bhogay mithiy ditith yath kande
ath kandi rozi sur na ta sas

O, You! Preoccupied with your body
O, You! Busy adorning it
Using it for pleasures and enjoyment
Not even dust and ashes will remain of this body

138

svamana garun manz yath kande
yath kandi dapan svarup nav
lubh muh tsaliy shub yiyi kande
yath kandi tiz tay sor prakash

Search for the Self within this body
This body is the abode of the Self
Forsaking greed and attachment will brighten
up your body
And it will illuminate like the sun

139

dyen tsezi ta razan ase
bhutal gaganas kun vikase
tsandri rah gros mavase
shiva puzan gvah tsitta atmase

The day will pass into night
The earth will reach out for the sky
The moon will swallow *Rahu*[39] on the day of
the new moon
Shiva's worship is the realization of the self
as consciousness

140

manasay man bhava saras
chyur kupa neryes narukh chokh
lyeka lyekh yudi tula koti
tuli tuli ta tul na kenh

Consider your mind like an ocean
If not restrained, fiery words will issue forth in anger
If weighed on a scale, these words will not have any weight

[39] *Rahu* is the demon of eclipse in Indian mythology.

141

cyeth amara pathi thavizi
ti travith lagi zude
tati tsa no shikizi sandarizi
dvada shur ta kvachi no mure

Focus your attention on the immortal path
If the mind strays from the path, it will be lost
Don't be afraid there, instead be courageous
A suckling baby is quiet in the lap

142

tsamar chathar ratha simhasan
hlad natye ras tula paryokh
kyah manith yeti sthir asavun
kozana kasiy maranani shankh

A fly-whisk, sunshade, chariot, and a throne
Merry making, pleasures of theater, or a soft bed
Think which of these will endure here
How can it relieve you of the fear of death?

143

mad pyuvum syandu zalan yut
rangan lilami karyem kaits
kati khyem manushi mamsaki nali
suy ba lal ta gauv me kyah

Wine I drank as the water of Sindhu
How many roles did I play on the stage of life
How many pieces of human flesh[40] did I eat
I am still the same Lalla
Nothing happened to me

144

raza hams asith sapadukh koluy
kustam tsoluy kyah tam hyeth
grata gauv band tay gratan hyot goluy
grata vol tsoluy phal phol hyeth

Even though a royal swan,
You have become mute
Someone has run away with something
As soon as the mill stopped
The grain channel got choked
The miller ran away with the grain[41]

[40] Lalla's reference to eating human flesh must not be taken literally. Eating human flesh is a metaphor for living out the material existence. The words "manushi mamsaki nali" could also represent an archaic expression whose meaning has been lost. Also see Grierson, p. 97.

[41] The word *hamsa* has two meanings: it refers to the basic meditation in the Shaiva tradition, but it also means the bird "swan" which is associated with beauty. Verse 144 is a metaphorical representation of spiritual experience. Even though humans have potential to reach an advanced state in the spiritual realm,

145

niyem karyoth garba
tsyetas karba pyeyiy
marana bronthay marba
marith ta martaba hariy

You made a vow in the womb
When will you remember that
Die before your death
Then on death you will attain to a higher state

146

karm za karan tre kombith
yeva labakh paralokas ankh
woth khas surya mandal tsombith
tavay tsaliy maranani shankh

Two types of actions—good and bad
Three are the causes [42]
Through *kumbhakha*, [43] you will find the other world
Arise and ascend piercing through the sun's disc
Then only will you lose the fear of death

---

yet they forget about it and hence, become impervious to this experience. Lalla compares it to the grinding mill that simply stops and the grain gets choked in the middle channel. Thus, indulging in worldly experiences leads to increasing entanglement. In such a state, Shiva, metaphorically represented by the owner of the mill, becomes inaccessible.

[42] Three types of causes are three types of impurities or *malas, (anavamala, mayiyamala, karmamala)* that lead to limited perception. See p. 72.

[43] *Kumbhakha* is a yogic practice that involves breath control.

147

kyah bodukh muha bhava sadari dare
soth lurith pyeyiy tam pankh
yemi bath kariney kali chora dare
kozana kasiy maranani shankh

Why have you immersed yourself in the sea of
illusory pleasures
Having destroyed the high banked road
You have got stuck in the mire
On the appointed time, death will take you
Who will relieve your fear of death

148

sutsasas na satas patsasas na rumas
su mas me lali cyauv panunuy vakh
andarim gatakah ratith ta volum
tsatith ta dyutamas tatiy cakh

I did not pause for the right moment
I did not trust anything
The wine I, Lalla, drank was my own verses
I caught the inner darkness, gathered it
Tearing it into shreds

Concordance of Various Lalla Collections

Jaishree Odin	Grierson & Barnett	Anand Koul	Jayalal Kaul	*Koshur Samachar*
1	98		5	2
2	106		1	1
3		12 (1930)	4	4
4	108		23	3
5	83		9	87
6	95		6	8
7	67		2	5
8		10 (1931)	87	29
9		25 (1930)	44	48
10	41		8	10
11	48		74	34
12	3		97	36
13	102		105	115 k
14	103		105	115kh
15	94		21	14
16		5 (1931)	24	13
17	60		99	37
18	49		86	35
19	13		128	114
20	8		73	46
21		15 (1933)	25	63
22	7		129	75
23		13 (1932)	43	54k
24		13 (1932)	42	54 kh
25		11 (1932)		56
26		24 (1932)	126	31
27		16 (1930)	123	113
28		20 (1930)		80
29		20 (1930)		80

Jaishree Odin	Grierson & Barnett	Anand Koul	Jayalal Kaul	*Koshur Samachar*
30	105		88	82
31	56		95	
32	57		96	141
33	101			20
34	69		91	21
35	59		135	110
36		1 (1931)		122
37	35		104	123
38	33		71	124
39	16		83	111
40	30		90	73
41	11		89	106
42	25		93	83
43	82		94	127
44	9		85	107
45	14		121	97
46	15		122	98
47	96		10	85
48	97		11	86
49	50		114	94
50	84			
51	85			
52		17 (1932)	46	52
53		16 (1932)	47	53
54		9 (1930)	125	116
55		17 (1932)	103	118
56		14 (1930)	58	119
57		5 (1930)	26	120
58	68		130	121
59	42		70	125

Jaishree Odin	Grierson & Barnett	Anand Koul	Jayalal Kaul	*Koshur Samachar*
60	93		137	133
61	109		127	131
62		12 (1933)	131	112
63	37		51	22
64	80		80	24
65	4		98	27
66	21		38	55
67		12 (1932)	75	81
68	31		100	130
69	44		136	132
70	58		138	134
71	65		110	76
72	78		119	95
73	79		120	96
74	39		68	42k
75	40		69	42kh
76		13 (1930)	14	6
77	18		39	57
78		23 (1932)	3	7
79	19		7	11
80	61		49	12
81	29		76	38
82		3 (1930)	116	
83		21 (1932)	57	105
84	45		67	43
85	1		133	108
86	2		134	109
87		23 (1930)	59	39
88	36		107	45
89	26		52	23
90		20 (1932)	63	25

Jaishree Odin	Grierson & Barnett	Anand Koul	Jayalal Kaul	*Koshur Samachar*
91		19 (1930)	65	44
92	72		29	40
93	88		35	33
94	76		102	129
95	5		132	74
96		4 (1930)	45	51
97		3 (1933)	50	32
98	51		77	99
99	52		78	100
100	53		79	102
101	46		84	104
102		31 (1930)	82	103
103	54		81	101
104	55		108	77
105		28 (1930)	124	72
106	107		15	16
107	63		62	17
108		2 (1931)		47
119	66		16	50
110	20		40	58
111		11 (1933)	28	28
112		27 (1932)	20	30
113	17		66	41
114		32 (1930)	18	157-158
115	28		33	60
116		10 (1933)	34	62
117		7 (1931)	27	64
118	27		30	65
119	12		48	66
120		17 (1930)	54	67a

Jaishree Odin	Grierson & Barnett	Anand Koul	Jayalal Kaul	*Koshur Samachar*
121			55	67kh
122	24		64	68
123	38		112	69
124	43		36	70
125	62		22	15
126	34		72	26
127	71		37	71
128	64		109	78
129	6		118	79
130	32		111	91
131		10 (1930)	56	92
132	47		113	93
133		6 (1930)		135
134	10		61	154
135	77		60	
136		7 (1930)	19	156
137		6 (1931)	31	59
138		6 (1931)	32	59
139	22		117	
140	23		41	
141	70		53	
142	73		12	
143	81		115	
144	86		106	
145	87		17	
146	75		101	
147	74		13	
148	104		92	

Bibliography

Translations and Commentaries of Lalla's Verses

Kaul, Jayalal. *Lal Ded.* New Delhi: Sahitya Akademi, 1973.

Koshur Samachar: A Socio-Cultural Monthly. Lalded Number. Vol. IX, No. 1 (Jan.–Feb. 1971), pp. 1–58.

Koul, Ananda. "Life Sketch of Laleshwari" and "Lalla-Vakyani". *The Indian Antiquary.* Vols. L (1921), pp. 309–12; LIX (1930), pp. 108–30; LX (1931), pp. 191–93; LXI (1932), pp. 13–16; LXII (1933), pp. 108–11.

Lal Ded: Her Life and Sayings. Trans., Nil Kanth Kotru. Srinagar: Utpal Publications, 1989.

Lalla-Vakyani: or The Wise Sayings of Lal Ded. Ed. and trans., Sir George Grierson and Lionell D. Barnett. London: Royal Asiatic Society, 1920.

Parimoo, B.N. *The Ascent of Self.* 2nd edn. Delhi: Motilal Banarsidass, 1987.

Temple, Richard Carnac. *The Religion and Teachings of Lalla.* New Delhi: Vintage Books, 1990.

The Wise Sayings of Laleshwari. Trans., S.N. Charagi. Srinagar: Trust Publishing House, 1938.

Philosophical Works on Kashmir Shaivism

Primary Sanskrit Sources

Iswarapratyabhijna of Utpaladeva. With the Vimarsini of Abhinavagupta. 2 vols.: Vol. I, ed. Mukund Ram Shastri; Vol. II, ed. Pandit Madhusudan Kaul Shastri. Kashmir Series of Texts and Studies,

Nos. XXII & XXXIII. Srinagar: Research Department, 1918, 1921.

Isvarapratyabhijna Vivritimarsini by Abhinavagupta. Vols. I, II, III. Ed., Pandit Madhusudan Kaul Shastri. Kashmir Series of Texts and Studies, Nos. LX, LXII, LXV. Srinagar: Research Department, 1918.

Malinivijayottara Tantram. Ed., Pandit Madhusudhan Kaul Shastri. Kashmir Series of Texts and Studies, No. XXXVII. Srinagar: Research Department, 1922.

Netratantram. With the Commentary Udyota of Ksemarajacarya. Ed., Pandit Vrajavallabh Dwivedi. Delhi: Parmal Publication, 1985.

Para-trimshika. With Commentary. The Latter by Abhinavagupta. Ed., Mahamahopadhyaya Pandit Mukunda Rama Shastri. Kashmir Series of Texts and Studies, No. XVIII. Srinagar: Research Department, 1918.

Shiva Sutra Vartika. By Bhaskara. Ed., Jagadisha Chandta Chatterji. Kashmir Series of Texts and Studies, No. IV. Srinagar: Research Department, 1916.

Shivasutra-Vartikam by Varadaraja. Ed., Pandit Madhusudan Kaul Shastri. Kashmir Series of Texts and Studies, No. XLIII. Srinagar: Research Department, 1925.

Shiva Sutra Vimarshini. Being the Sutras of Vasu Gupta with the Commentary Called Vimarshini by Ksemaraja. Ed., J.C. Chatterji. Kashmir Series of Texts and Studies, No. 1. Srinagar: Research Department, 1921.

Sivadrsti of Srisomanandanatha. With the Vritti by Utpaladeva. Ed., Pandit Madhusudan Kaul Shastri. Kashmir Series of Texts and Studies, No. LIV. Sringar: Research Department, 1934.

Spanda Karikas. With the Vivriti of Ramakantha. Ed., J.C. Chatterji. Kashmir Series of Texts and Studies, No. VI. Srinagar: Research Department, 1913.

Spanda Karikas. With the Vritti by Kallata. Ed., J.C.Chatterji. Kashmir Series of Texts and Studies, No. V. Srinagar: Research Department, 1916.

Spandakarikas of Vasugupta. With the Nirnaya by Ksemaraja. Ed. and trans., Pandit Madhusudan Kaul Shastri. Kashmir Series of Texts and Studies, No. XLII. Srinagar: Research Department, 1925.

The Svacchandatantram. With Commentary Udyota by Ksemarajacarya. Ed., Pandit Vraj Vallabh Dwivedi. Vols. I, II. Delhi: Parimal Publications, 1985.

Tantraloka of Abhinava Gupta. With Commentary by Rajanaka Jayaratha. 13 vols. Vol. I: ed., Mahamahopadhyaya Pandit Mukund Ram Shastri; Vol XII: ed., Pandit Mukunda Kaul Shastri. Kashmir Series of Texts and Studies, Nos. XXIII and LVIII. Srinagar: Research Department, 1918, 1937.

Sanskrit Works in Translation

The Aphorisms of Siva: The Siva Sutra with Bhaskara's Commentary, the Varttika. Trans., Mark S.G. Dyczkowski. New York: SUNY Press, 1992.

Pratyabhijnanhrdayam: The Secret of Self Recognition. Trans., Jaideva Singh. Delhi: Motilal Banarsidass, 1979.

Siva Sutras: The Yoga of Supreme Identity. Trans., Jaideva Singh. Delhi: Motilal Banarsidass, 1979.

The Siva Purana. Vols. 1–4. Ed., J. L. Shastri. Delhi: Motilal Banarsidass, 1995.

Spanda Karikas. Trans., Jaideva Singh. Delhi: Motilal Banarsidass, 1980.

The Stanzas on Vibration. Trans., Mark S. G. Dyczkowski. New York: SUNY Press, 1992.

Vijnanabhairava or Divine Consciousness. Trans., Jaideva Singh. Delhi: Motilal Banarsidass, 1979.

Works on Indian Aesthetics

Chaudhury, Pravas Jivan. "The Aesthetic Attitude in Indian Aesthetics". *The Journal of Aesthetics and Art Criticism* (Fall 1965), pp. 145–217.

The Dhvanyaloka of Anandavardhana. With the Locana of Abhinavagupta. Trans., Daniel H. H. Ingalls, Jeffrey M. Masson and M.V. Patwardhan. Massachusetts: Harvard University Press, 1990.

Gnoli, Raniero. *The Aesthetic Experience According to Abhinavagupta.*

Varanasi: Chowkhamba Sanskrit Series Office, 1985.

Masson, J.L. and M.V. Patwardhan. *Santarasa and Abhinavagupta's Philosophy of Aesthetics*, 1969. Poona: Bhandarkar Oriental Research Institute, 1985.

Natyasastra of Bharatamuni. With the Commentary Abhinavabharati by Abhinavaguptacarya. Ed., R. S. Nagar. Delhi: Parimal Publications, 1981.

Pandey, K. C. *Comparative Aesthetics*. Vol. I. Varanasi: Chowkhamba Sanskrit Series Office, 1959.

Sastri, P.S. *Indian Theory of Aesthetics*. Delhi: Bharariya Vidya Prakashan, 1989.

Hanumantha Rao, G. *Comparative Aesthetics: Eastern and Western*. Mysore: Mysore Printing and Publishing House, 1974.

Walimbe, Y.S. *Abhinavagupta on Indian Aesthetics*. Delhi: Ajanta Publications, 1980.

Related Works on Philosophy, Religion, Poetry, History

Altekar, A.S. *The Position of Women in Hindu Civilization*. Delhi: Motilal Banarsidass, 1991.

Akbar, M.J. *Kashmir: Behind the Vale*. New Delhi, Viking 1991.

Bailly, Constantina Rhodes. *Shaiva Devotional Songs of Kashmir: A Translation and Study of Utpaladeva's Shivastotravali*. Albany, New York: SUNY Press, 1987.

Bamzai, Prithvi Nath Kaul. *A History of Kashmir*. Delhi: Metropolitan Book Co, 1962.

Bazaz, P.N. *Daughters of the Vitasta*. New Delhi: Pamposh Publications, 1959.

Bhagavad Gita. Trans. Sri Swami Sivananda. Durban: Sivananda Press, 1983.

Bhattacharya, N.N. *The Indian Mother Goddess*. New Delhi: Manohar, 1977.

Bohm, David. *Wholeness and the Implicate Order*. London: Routledge and Kegan Paul, 1980.

Chatterji, J.C. *Kashmir Shaivism*. Albany, New York: SUNY Press, 1982.

Chatterji, J.C. *Kashmir Shaivism.* Albany, New York: SUNY Press, 1982.

Chodorow, Nancy. *The Reproduction of Mothering.* Berkeley: University of California Press, 1978.

Coburn, Thomas B. *Encountering the Goddess: A Translation of the Devi-Mahatmaya and a Study of Its Interpretation.* Albany, New York: SUNY Press, 1991.

Daly, Mary. *Beyond God the Father.* Boston: Beacon Press, 1978.

Dallery, Arleen B. "The Politics of Writing (the) Body: Ecriture Feminine" in *Gender/Body/Knowledge: Feminist Reconstructions of Being and Knowing.* Eds. Alison M. Jaggar and Susan R. Bordo. New Brunswick, New Jersey: Rutgers University Press, 1992.

Dhar, Triloki Nath. *Rupa Bhawani: Life, Teachings, and Philosophy.* Srinagar: Valley Printing Press, 1977.

Dimen, Muriel. "Power, Sexuality and Intimacy" in *Gender/Body/Knowledge: Feminist Reconstructions of Being and Knowing.* Eds. Alison M. Jaggar and Susan R. Bordo. New Brunswick, New Jersey: Rutgers University Press, 1992.

Drabu, Vishva Nath. *Saivagamas.* New Delhi: Indus Publishing Company, 1990.

Dyczkowski, Mark S. G. *The Doctrine of Vibration: An Analysis of the Doctrines and Practices of Kashmir Shaivism.* New York: SUNY Press, 1987.

Erndl, Kathleen M. *Victory to the Mother.* New York and Oxford: Oxford University Press, 1993.

Flood, Gavin. *Body and Cosmology in Kashmir Saivism.* San Francisco: Mellon Research University Press, 1993.

Hasan, Mohibbul. *Kashmir Under the Sultans.* Calcutta: Iran Society, 1959.

Irigaray, Luce. *Speculum of the Other Woman.* Trans. Gillian C. Gill. Ithaca, New York: Cornell University Press, 1994.

Irigaray, Luce. *This Sex which is not One.* Trans. Catherine Porter with Carolyn Burke. New York: Cornell University Press, 1985.

Irigaray, Luce. *An Ethics of Sexual Difference.* Trans. Carolyn Bruke and Gillian C. Gill. New York: Cornell University Press, 1993.

Jonaraja. *Rajatarangini of Jonaraja*. Trans. Jogesh Chunder Dutt. Delhi: Gian Publishing House, 1986.

Jones, Serene. "This God Which Is Not One: Irigaray and Barth on the Divine" in *Transfigurations: Theology and the French Feminists*. Eds. C.W. Maggie Kim, Susan M. St. Ville and Susan M. Simonaitis. Minneapolis: Fortress Press, 1993.

Kachru, Braj B. *Kashmiri Literature*. Wiesbaden: Otto Harrassowitz, 1981.

Kak, Ram Nath. *Autumn Leaves*. New Delhi: Vitasta Publications, 1996.

Kak, Subhash C. "On the Science of Consciousness in Ancient India." *Indian Journal of History of Science*, 32 (2), 1997.

Kalhana. *Rajatarangini*. Trans. R.S. Pandit. New Delhi: Sahitya Akademi, 1990.

Kalhana. *Rajatarngini*. Trans. M.A. Stein. Vols I & II. Delhi: Motilal Banarsidass, 1961.

Kinsley, David. *Hindu Goddesses*. Delhi: Motilal Banarsidass, 1987.

Keller, Catherine. *From a Broken Web*. Boston: Beacon Press, 1986.

Kramrisch, Stella. *The Presence of Siva*. Princeton, N.J.: Princeton University Press, 1981.

Kumar, Pushpendra. *Sakti Cult in Ancient India*. Varanasi: Bhartiya Publishing House, 1974.

Lakshman Jee, Swami. *Kashmir Saivism: The Secret Supreme*. New York: SUNY Press, 1988.

Laws of Manu. Trans. Wendy Doniger & Brian K. Smith. New York: Penguin, 1992.

Leslie, Julia I. *The Perfect Wife*. Delhi: Oxford University Press, 1989.

Madan, T.N. *Family and Kinship: A Study of the Pandits of Rural Kashmir*. Delhi: Oxford University Press, 1989.

Maslow, Abraham H. *Toward a Psychology of Being*. Princeton, N.J.: Van Nostrand, 1968.

Mishra, Kamalkar. *Kashmir Saivism: The Central Philosophy of Tantrism*. Cambridge, Ma: Rudra Press, 1993.

Muktananda, Swami. *Play of Consciousness*. San Francisco: Harper and Row, 1978.

Muller-Ortega, Paul Eduardo. *The Triadic Heart of Siva*. Albany, New York: SUNY Press, 1989.

O'Flaherty, Wendy Doniger. *Asceticism and Eroticism in the Mythology of Siva*. London: Oxford University Press, 1973.

Pandit, B. N. *Aspects of Kashmir Saivism*. Srinagar: Utpal Publication. 1977.

Pandit, B. N. *History of Kashmir Saivism*. Srinagar: Utpal Publication, 1990.

Pintchman, Tracy. *The Rise of the Goddess in the Hindu Tradition*. New York: SUNY Press, 1994.

Rastogi, Navjivan. *The Krama Tantricism of Kashmir*. Vol. I. Delhi: Motilal Banarsidass, 1979.

Ramanujan, A. K. *Speaking of Shiva*. Maryland, U.S.A.: Penguin, 1973.

Ray, S. C. *Early History and Culture in Kashmir*. Delhi, India: Motilal Banarsidass, 1969.

Roy, Kumkum. "Defining the Household: Some Aspects of Prescription and Practice in Early India" *Social Scientist*. Vol. 22, No. 1, 1994.

Silburn, Lilian. *Kundalini: The Energy of the Depths*. Trans. Jacques Gontier. New York: SUNY Press, 1988.

Sangari, Kumkum. "Consent, Agency and Rhetorics of Incitement" in *Economic and Political Weekly*. May 1, 1993.

Sangari, Kumkum. "Mirabai and the Spiritual Economy of *Bhakti*". *Economic and Political Weekly*. July 7, 1990.

Shrivara's *Jainarajatarangini* in *Medieval Kashmir*. Ed. S. L. Sadhu. Reprint of the J.C. Dutta's translation of *Rajtaranginis* of Jonaraja, Shrivara and Shuka (published in 1898 AD under the title *Kings of Kashmira* Vol III). New Delhi: Atlantic Publishers, 1993.

Stein, Aurel. Introduction in *Kalhana's Rajatarangini or the Chronicle of the Kings of Kasmir*. Vol 1. Delhi: Motilal Banarsidass, 1961.

Sufi, G.M.D. *Kashir: A History of Kashmir*. 2 vols. New Delhi: Light and Life publishers, 1974.

Swamy, H. Thipperudra. *The Virasaiva Saints: A Study*. Trans. S. M. Angadi. Mysore: Rao and Raghavan, 1968.

Weil, Kari. *Androgyny and the Denial of Difference*. Charlottesville and London: University Press of Virginia, 1992.

Whitford, Margaret. *Luce Iragaray: Philosophy in the Feminine*. London and New York: Routledge, 1991.

Woodroffe, John. *Sakti and Sakta*. Madras: Ganesh and Company, 1987.

Index